in real life

From the Foreword

by Dr. Laura Schlessinger

"Every one of us has lived through moments when we were caught up in some particularly moving experience, spiritual epiphany, sobering revelation, cosmic wake-up call, character-defining incident, overwhelming challenge, humorous distraction, or ironic comeuppance. We all have stories of instants when we glimpsed stupidity, evil, or cruel selfishness; when we experienced the grandeur of human decency and compassion; or when we simply received a reminder of the beauty of life, that ever-so-brief gift.

"In this little book you'll find a rich sampling of all of the above. Amidst this wonderful variety of stories, there are two common threads. The first is that all of the stories are true; you won't be reading Hollywood fantasies in the pages ahead, but rather genuine chronicles of incredible moments from the actual lives of real American men and women.

"The second thing connecting all these stories is that it's impossible to read any one of them without feeling as if we've become familiar with the writer—personally. When reading heartfelt and well-written personal stories like these, we're never alone: We connect with people all over the world, through all time. It's both exhilarating and enlightening to relive these human moments through the perceptions of others. That the stories are true makes them even more riveting and important than a fictitious tale would be. Our own lives are expanded and deepened by the sharing of these hard-won experiences."

Also by Karl Zinsmeister

BOOTS ON THE GROUND:
A Month with the 82nd Airborne in the Battle for Iraq

DAWN OVER BAGHDAD:
How the U.S. Military
Is Using Bullets and Ballots to Remake Iraq

Other New Beginnings Press Titles

By Ben Stein and Phil DeMuth

CAN AMERICA SURVIVE?
The Rage of the Left, the Truth, and What to Do about It

YES, YOU CAN BE A
SUCCESSFUL INCOME INVESTOR!
Reaching for Yield in Today's Market

YES, YOU CAN STILL RETIRE COMFORTABLY!
The Baby-Boom Retirement Crisis and How to Beat It

All of the above are available at your local bookstore,
or may be ordered by visiting the distributors
for New Beginnings Press:

Hay House USA: **www.hayhouse.com**
Hay House Australia: **www.hayhouse.com.au**
Hay House UK: **www.hayhouse.co.uk**
Hay House South Africa: **orders@psdprom.co.za**

in real life
powerful lessons from everyday living

Edited by **Karl Zinsmeister**
with Karina Rollins

NBP

NEW BEGINNINGS PRESS
Carlsbad, California

Copyright © 2005 by the American Enterprise Institute

Published by: New Beginnings Press, Carlsbad, California

Distributed in the USA by: Hay House, Inc., P.O. Box 5100, Carlsbad, CA 92018-5100 • *Phone:* (760) 431-7695 or (800) 654-5126 • *Fax:* (760) 431-6948 or (800) 650-5115 • www.hayhouse.com • *Distributed in Australia by:* Hay House Australia Pty. Ltd., 18/36 Ralph St., Alexandria NSW 2015 • *Phone:* 612-9669-4299 • *Fax:* 612-9669-4144 • www.hayhouse.com.au • *Distributed in the United Kingdom by:* Hay House UK, Ltd. • Unit 62, Canalot Studios • 222 Kensal Rd., London W10 5BN • *Phone:* 44-20-8962-1230 • *Fax:* 44-20-8962-1239 • www. hayhouse.co.uk • *Distributed in the Republic of South Africa by:* Hay House SA (Pty), Ltd., P.O. Box 990, Witkoppen 2068 • *Phone/Fax:* 27-11-706-6612 • orders@psdprom.co.za • *Distributed in Canada by:* Raincoast • 9050 Shaughnessy St., Vancouver, B.C. V6P 6E5 • *Phone:* (604) 323-7100 • *Fax: (604) 323-2600*

Editorial supervision: Jill Kramer • *Design:* Amy Rose Szalkiewicz

Library of Congress Cataloging-in-Publication Data

In real life : powerful lessons from everyday living / edited by Karl Zinsmeister ; with Karina Rollins.
  p. cm.
  ISBN-13: 978-1-4019-0752-5
  ISBN-10: 1-4019-0752-0
  1. Conduct of life. 2. Success. I. Zinsmeister, Karl. II. Rollins, Karina.
  BJ1521.I6 2005
  170'.44--dc22   2005004977

ISBN 13: 978-1-4019-0752-5
ISBN 10: 1-4019-0752-0

08 07 06 05   4 3 2 1
1st printing, August 2005

Printed in the United States of America

Dedicated
to the loyal readers
and talented writers of
The American Enterprise
magazine

Contents

THE GREAT INDOORS

Foreword

The True Riches of Reality

Laura Schlessinger, Ph.D., the author of eight best-selling nonfiction books and four children's books, dispenses advice for real life every weekday on her internationally syndicated radio program.

Every one of us has lived through moments when we were caught up in some particularly moving experience, spiritual epiphany, sobering revelation, cosmic wake-up call, character-defining incident, overwhelming challenge, humorous distraction, or ironic comeuppance. We all have stories of instants when we glimpsed stupidity, evil, or cruel selfishness;

when we experienced the grandeur of human decency and compassion; or when we simply received a reminder of the beauty of life, that ever-so-brief gift.

In this little book you'll find a rich sampling of all of the above. Amidst this wonderful variety of stories, there are two common threads. The first is that all of the stories are true; you won't be reading Hollywood fantasies in the pages ahead, but rather genuine chronicles of incredible moments from the actual lives of real American men and women.

The second thing connecting all these stories is that it's impossible to read any one of them without feeling as if we've become familiar with the writer—personally. When reading heartfelt and well-written personal stories like these, we're never alone: We connect with people all over the world, through all time. It's both exhilarating and enlightening to relive these human moments through the perceptions of others. That the stories are true makes them even more riveting and important than a fictitious tale would be. Our own lives are expanded and deepened by the sharing of these hard-won experiences.

Today there are lots of television programs that pretend to present "reality." Their producers try to tap in to this immediacy and emotional power I've just described. But instead of real life as normal and admirable people live it, these programs use contrived and horrible personal situations. In shows such as *Wife Swap, The Osbournes,* and *Growing Up Gotti,* individuals exploit their children, spouses, strangers, and themselves in return for 15 minutes of fame and lots of money.

It's sad that ratings are now earned heavily through these so-called reality shows, which reward participants for betraying, humiliating, and demeaning each other. We know that the audience for these programs is primarily young, which portends nothing good for the moral tenor and aesthetic taste of our upcoming generations. Such programming teaches children that human beings are fodder for gross entertainment, rather than sacred beings made in the image of God. They encourage adults to degrade themselves for the amusement of voyeurs. And they build audiences who enjoy seeing people in fear, pain, or jeopardy.

A much more accurate, gripping, and wholesome type of reality can be found in the stories within these pages. They're about real people confronting real situations, conveying real reactions, and having real insights. True, many of them will leave you *feeling* better about life, although that isn't the point. The point of life is to *become* better by virtue of having been touched by the spirit and insight of another human.

Feeling better doesn't necessarily lead us to *being* better. In fact, doing the right thing often has a price attached, and that may not feel so good at the time. It's that still, small voice of ingrained values—and the reinforcement of those values by benevolent, respected, and like-minded folks—which gives us the strength to be good when it would feel better to be a bad person. These stories provide just that kind of reinforcement.

Now, it's my turn. I have a story—a true story.

At the end of my freshman year of college, I was seriously burned out. For most of my growing-up years, my father had put outrageous pressure on me, continually telling me that I was lazy and stupid. I did just okay in high school, although it was quite apparent to my teachers that my abilities far outweighed my academic performance. With just a little over a B average, I got into a great college solely on the basis of my interview. (I remember the college recruiter enjoying our discussions about science, philosophy, and so forth, and then stopping to look at my very average grades, perplexed.)

When I enrolled in college, I moved into a dormitory and out of my parents' home, which was both a blessing and a curse. The blessing was that on my own, I was able to work up to my potential. For the four years I was in school, I was never off the dean's list, and I had a position of responsibility as a laboratory assistant in the biology department.

The curse, however, was that I worked myself into psychological and emotional exhaustion. At the end of that first year of college, I felt unglued. So, in an attempt to do something completely different, I took a nonpaying summer job at a school/rehabilitation center for the physically handicapped. While it was emotionally draining to see the suffering of children and adults, many of whom had terminal handicaps, it was wonderful helping kids learn science, while also coping with the slings and arrows of my patients' real lives.

The pivotal experience for me was the two weeks I spent training in the adult rehabilitation center. I was paired with a 30-year-old black man who'd only recently recovered from a car crash, which had left him confined to a wheelchair, paralyzed permanently from the waist down. His current rehab assignment was learning to sort transistors. He couldn't go back to his previous job, so he needed to learn some new way to support himself.

For most of the first week we sorted and chatted, sorted and chatted, sorted and chatted, for eight hours a day. Then one day, bored to tears, I mindlessly chortled, "This is soooo boring!"

The second I finished, I wished I could have sucked the words back out of the air. No such luck.

He turned to me, stared, and responded patiently, teaching the "teacher" an important lesson in life. He told me that he'd once been an athlete with unlimited potential, and now he was a paraplegic with a long list of things that he was simply unable to do. He agreed that what we were doing was boring. But then he said, *"Anything* in life can become boring, even those things that seemed so exciting at the beginning. The key is to do whatever you do with meaning. The bosses told me to do this job a certain way and declared that only a certain amount could be finished in the time allotted. My job is not to 'sort.' My job is to find a way to do this better and faster—to break the limits. My creativity and sweat take this boring task and make it a challenge for me."

I vividly remember the feeling I had at that very moment: It was a mixture of shame—for my thoughtless comment about what I'd seen as this man's pitiable current work situation, as well as for my lack of insight—and excitement at the notion that any assignment can become a meaningful challenge. This wise man and I spent the rest of our time together experimenting with new and better ways to sort, handle, and count those transistors.

Going back to college at the end of that summer had me looking forward to creating my own challenges—instead of just fighting off the real and perceived ones from my father, which had exhausted me. My friend in the wheelchair helped me guide my life toward something much more positive. I'd like to say that it only took this one lesson, but I'd be fibbing. Yet having this story inside my mind regularly gives me benevolent (though sometimes bittersweet) reminders to straighten out my thinking. Just when my attitude gets mopey and out of whack, that experience, or some other tale I've lived or assimilated from others, will pop in my mind and help me get back on track.

Who knows who I'd be and what I'd be doing had that simple, awkward, helpful little moment not occurred? Hmm . . . one small human encounter really *can* change a life.

Oftentimes an interviewer will ask me about mentors, role models, and so forth. I guess they're expecting me to name prominent individuals in radio or psychotherapy, or the usual personal suspects like parents or teachers. But many of the most pivotal moments in my life arose from seemingly "incidental" interactions that took place right amidst my humble daily routines. I bet I'm not alone in that. Think about the things that have nudged your life in a different direction.

The real-life stories in this book are wonderful examples of the kinds of "happenings" that can open a fresh door on your thinking. My hope is that you'll be so inspired by them that you'll share your own similar stories with others. For it is in the honest telling, and hearing, of real-life stories that keeps all humanity connected.

Human experience in life is not like a physical resource that runs low as you give it away. Sharing our tales, as this book does so beautifully, elevates rather than impoverishes the giver—but it elevates the recipient even more.

— **Dr. Laura Schlessinger**
Santa Barbara, California

Opening

Private Pictures Paint a National Portrait

I run a national magazine based in Washington, D.C., and New York called *The American Enterprise*. It's a serious publication about current affairs, and in every installment we wrestle with tricky political topics, economic subjects, questions of war and peace, and issues of the future. Contributors ranging from Rudy Giuliani to Clint Eastwood to physicist Freeman Dyson to Dick and Lynne Cheney appear in our pages.

But right from our launch in 1995, we've insisted on including in our editorial mix a little department we call "In Real Life." Here, we invite ordinary people to talk to us about interesting twists in their weekly existence. It might be a cop describing a rough arrest he'd just made, someone recounting the day his life was saved by a friend, a divinity student mourning the politicization of fellow students, a mother explaining why she homeschools her child, or an athlete reliving a brutal contest.

The common thread in these short slices of life is that they're all true. They describe real people, real events, real struggles, and real triumphs—in the workplace, at home, and in the stormy bosom of an individual's soul. Not surprisingly, these little tales have proven to be a very popular part of our magazine.

While these narratives vary as wildly as the personalities who tell them, it's been intriguing to watch certain themes bubble up repeatedly over the years—for example, discovering how much more there is to life than the material; the gratitude for good fortune and unearned blessings that hits many of us as we age; reveling in the pleasures of nature; learning the penalties of selfishness the hard way; and finding that success in one's family life trumps almost any other satisfaction. Time and again we at the magazine get glimpses of deep, universal hungers: for human trust and love, for excellence, for friendship, and for a connection to God. These are the driving forces behind millions of everyday lives.

For this book, my fellow editors and I decided to organize some of the stories we've published into three sections:

— *Interior Monologues* collects very personal reflections (a soldier's homecoming, the death of a childhood friend, a struggle against heroin addiction, the joy of an adoption, butterflies upon sending a child to college, and so forth).

— *The Great Outdoors* includes some great "guy" themes (the aches and pains of a softball league or spring cattle branding, the pleasure of dogs, the rumble of a pickup truck on an open road, vivid fishing and hunting tales, and lots of sports), but also some more poignant fare—including near-death experiences (under the ice in a raging creek, being shot at) and post-death experiences (a guard at the Tomb of the Unknown Soldier describing his solemn duty).

— *The Great Indoors* chronicles house fires, fast-food jobs, and weddings (from the point of view of the bride's father). It includes a painful story of a bittersweet night in a hotel bar, along with the true tale of a distinctly un-handy dad who nonetheless helps his son build a winning Pinewood Derby car.

The subjects covered by the essays in this book are ultimately far more important to most Americans than the news events, financial minutiae, and celebrity gossip that flood our airwaves, periodicals, and other media. But these are very personal topics that are difficult to talk about honestly with strangers, so the kinds of admissions and yearnings collected in these pages are rare in public life—even though they make up some of the most intense and meaningful parts of our private lives.

We decided to breach that boundary between the personal and the public. By compiling these wonderful, blunt, emotional, personal stories into book form, we hope that they can be read, enjoyed, mulled over, and profited from by thousands of new readers (a nice little service to humanity). After all, people can—and regularly do—learn from the personal victories and private mistakes of others.

In that sense, we hope that this book, in addition to bringing amused smiles and knowing sighs to readers, can help make our collective cultural life a little more wholesome. For one of the great untold stories of the last generation in America is that, in general, our society is in ascendance, not decline. You'd never know it by what often dominates our TV screens, but the fact is, the health and strength of our country, and the quality and happiness of our individual lives, have both clearly improved (on average) over the last two decades.

I'm not claiming that present-day America is heaven on earth. There are still addicts and criminals, depressing schools, too many broken families, and citizens with shut minds and hardened hearts in our land. But on the subjects that form the backdrop for most of the personal stories in this book—family life, satisfaction with work, spiritual awareness, the quality of childhood, and so forth—many heartening mid-course corrections have recently taken place.

Consider some of the ways in which our collective lives have become better, stabler, sunnier, and saner over the last generation (as demonstrated in government statistics, academic research, and polling):

- Our suicide rate has tumbled more than 20 percent from the levels of the 1970s and early '80s.

- Binge drinking among high schoolers has reached record lows, and drug use is also down.

- Since peaking in 1991, the violent crime rate has fallen by a third, to a 30-year low.

- Today's fathers are much more involved in home-building tasks than their predecessors, and compared to baby boomers, Gen-X mothers are *twice* as likely to spend the majority of their day "attending to child rearing" while their offspring are young.

- While 25 years ago only 40 percent of teenagers told pollsters that they had "no serious family problems," today the figure is up to 80 percent.

- Teen pregnancy has also dropped to its lowest recorded level—down from 117 per 1,000 girls in 1990 to 84 in 2000. This isn't just a matter of better contraception. The number of teens postponing sex has increased rapidly from a minority to a majority. Between 1995 and 2002, the fraction of teenage boys who were sexually active declined from 55 to 46 percent. Fully 92 percent of teenagers now say that it's important for them to "get strong messages from society that they shouldn't have sex until they're at least out of high school."

- The divorce rate in the U.S. turned a corner in 1981 and has since fallen by 25 percent.

- The abortion rate in the U.S. also topped out in 1981 and has since fallen by more than 25 percent.

- 93 percent of college seniors now say that they plan to marry (or already have), and they hope to have an average of three children. Both of these figures are sharp rebounds from the previous generation.

- The number of welfare recipients in the U.S. peaked in 1993 at 14.2 million, and has since tumbled to 5.4 million.

- The poverty level of black Americans has fallen by 25 percent over the last ten years.

- The high school dropout rate is now 21 percent lower than it was in 1975.

- The American work ethic is thriving: The fraction of the adult population holding down a job has risen from 57 percent in the 1970s to 64 percent today.

- Our charitable impulse is also alive and well. In constant, inflation-adjusted dollars, the average annual donation to charity in the U.S. has risen from $464 to $748 per person.

- Today's young Americans are described by experts as "the most entrepreneurial generation in American history." Fully 80 percent of the individuals starting new businesses today are between the ages of 19 and 31.

- The number of college freshmen describing themselves as conservatives now equals the portion calling themselves liberals. A generation ago, self-described liberals outnumbered conservatives three to one.

- Survey research shows that religious belief and churchgoing are both up since the early 1990s.

Think of the essays in this book as little photographs that, if put together in mosaic fashion, give you many flesh-and-blood hints of the kinds of broad social change documented in the cold statistics above. In that sense, this book is a sociological portrait as well as a work of literature. In the process of telling crystalline little real-life human stories, it also outlines some of the important new paths that we as a nation have traveled over the last generation.

I want to thank the essayists who contributed to this book (a few favorites appear more than once) for not only entertaining us, but also helping bring these big societal shifts to life via their own private stories. Through their openness, honesty, sensitivity, and humor, they help us realize that we're not alone—in our happinesses or our hurts.

I also want to thank several editors who helped me find and shape these stories in the years since we started publishing them in 1995, particularly Scott Walter and Karina Rollins (Karina also assisted in selecting and ordering these tales from an abundance of riches). And please note that all of these contributions, which originally appeared in *The American Enterprise,* have been specially re-edited for book publication.

This was an enjoyable and very satisfying project to put together. At some level, rereading these accounts helped bolster my faith in humanity. May it have the same effect on you.

— **Karl Zinsmeister**
Cazenovia, New York

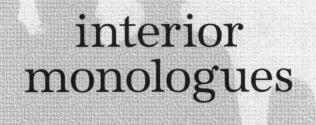

interior
monologues

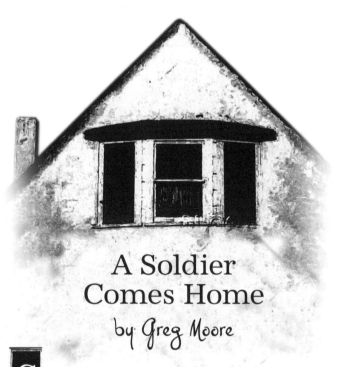

A Soldier
Comes Home
by Greg Moore

SARANAC LAKE, NEW YORK, JANUARY 2005: There are no longer generators running, armored vehicles rumbling, or mortars exploding, and the roar of the silence is deafening to me. What I hear at night now is the gentle breaths released from the perfect lips of my sons. The same lips that I cannot kiss enough. The lips that make my eyes fill with tears every time they touch my cheeks.

My release from Fort Drum came earlier than expected, so when I pulled into my driveway at noon, the house was empty. I dropped my bags inside and walked alone through the rooms, soaking in the images and smells that had only been a memory during ten months in Iraq.

My oldest son's first-grade teacher had been wonderful to me while I was away. She sent updates and pictures via e-mail almost weekly. So when I popped my head into her classroom, she came running and gave me a "welcome home" hug.

"Easton is practicing a song," she said. "Why don't you surprise him?"

My heart was racing. I followed the sound of the piano and the little voices singing, then stood and watched. Trickles of love and pride started streaming involuntarily down my cheeks as I listened to my son, who'd gotten so big. The anticipation built as I waited for him to see me.

The little girl next to him was the first to notice the uniformed man standing in the doorway. The image she saw and the facts she'd been told were doing battle in her brain. Then her eyes grew wide and her mouth fell open. "Easton, Easton—your Daddy's here!" she practically squealed.

My son's head snapped around. The excitement and disbelief on his face is something I'll never forget. I motioned him to come to me, and he ran into my open arms. There was no hiding my tears, and I didn't care to. This was the day I'd been waiting for.

I choked out my words of love and hung on to this boy who had cried so many nights, who'd said that he didn't care if he got any other presents for Christmas—he only wanted his Daddy to come home. This boy, who'd used up all his wishes on me, kept pulling his head back from my shoulder to look at my face. Cheers rose from the teachers and the other kids.

Hand-in-hand, Easton and I stepped outside and drove to the other side of town. I had another little boy to catch up with. When I went inside, he was napping. "Marshall, wake up. I have a surprise for you," I heard his day-care provider say.

He came out with his head on her shoulder. When he looked up, his eyes grew wide and all signs of sleepiness disappeared. "Daddy!" he exclaimed in pure excitement, as he fell forward into my arms. My heart ached with love, and pure joy soaked my cheeks once again.

I was complete now. I had my boys. And there have never been more perfect words spoken to me than "I love you, Dad."

It may take my wife and children a long time to realize that while I may look it, I'm not the same person who said good-bye to them many months ago. I'll never be the same again—and thankfully so.

Each day now I'm acutely aware of what makes me happy, and what it is I do that makes others feel that way. Walking through the volatile streets in Iraq helped me see this much more clearly, and I'll make every effort to preserve that awareness for the rest of my days.

When I look through my photo album, I think about the men I served with and learned to count on, who are no longer by my side. The men who had their bodies pierced by the hatred of terrorists, who left their last breath in a place far away—great men doing a job that allows this noble country the freedoms it deserves.

I've seen the dark side of humanity, and it has forever changed me. As I sit here in my home, with the sun streaming through the windows, I look out and see the boughs of the evergreens blowing in the breeze. There are no armed guards on the roof. Sandbags are nowhere to be found. No longer do I call in grid coordinates of my whereabouts.

Mission briefs have been replaced by wonderful communication between two parents. As I drive through town, I'm alone, with no turret and no gunner above me. I don't have to scrutinize every pile of dirt or plastic bag for fear that it may explode.

Amazingly, I am safe.

Greg Moore is a staff sergeant in the New York National Guard's 2nd Battalion, 108th Infantry.

A Reunion

by Karina Rollins

WASHINGTON, D.C., SEPTEMBER 2002: Andrea and I were best friends in grade school. True best buddies—the kind where you're virtually inseparable, where classmates ask, "Where's your friend?" if they see you alone. Spending the night at each other's home was the greatest treat.

We attended an American school in Germany, where our fathers were both stationed with the military. After fifth grade, Andrea's dad was sent back to the States. She promised that she'd write as soon as she knew her permanent address.

¶

I waited . . . and waited. The letter never came. At some point, my father, through military channels, was able to get her family's address. But by the time I tried to reach her, that address was no longer valid. This was in the days before e-mail and the wonders of the Internet, and options for a 13-year-old hoping to find a lost friend were limited. After several years, I accepted that I wouldn't hear from Andrea. But I never forgot her, and I always wondered, *Why?*

The first time I came to live in the U.S. was in 1989, when I moved to Maryland for my last two years of college. Shortly after I arrived, I resumed my search for my erstwhile best friend by calling directory assistance: first in Georgia, where I knew she'd lived for a while, and then I tried other states with big military bases, like Texas and North Carolina. Nothing.

Fast-forward to 1996. I'm living in New York, made the leap to the cyber age. My colleagues and I crowded around the computers to try out the Internet.

Still a bit bewildered about exactly what we should be trying to do on this great World Wide Web, a co-worker stumbled across phone-book listings for the entire country, available right there at our fingertips. "Anyone want to find someone?" he asked. And then it hit me. "Yes," I said, "I'm looking for my best friend."

Andrea could have married and changed her last name, but I'd always remembered her father's name, complete with middle initial, so we tried that first. A single address matched: It was in Seattle. Could this be it? I called the number right away. A machine came on announcing that I'd reached "Harry and Sabine." Sabine? Yes, that was her mom's name, wasn't it? I left a message—still, I didn't dare to hope.

When I came home that night, I found a note from my roommate telling me that a Sabine from Seattle had called and was very excited to talk to me. A shiver ran through my body; then I became giddy and danced around the living room. I'd actually found her! My fingers trembled as I dialed the number 3,000 miles away.

A friendly woman answered, and I announced it was me. "Karina!" she exclaimed. "How are you, dear? How did you find us?"

My mind reeled. It had been 17 years. Overwhelmed, all I could do was babble, "Is it you? Is it really you?"

"Yes, of course it's me!" Andrea's mother, Sabine, exclaimed. She asked me where I lived, what my job was like, and how my mother was doing. I answered dutifully, but my brain was pounding: *What about Andrea? Why doesn't she say something about Andrea?*

The longer we talked, a feeling of horrible, terrible dread started to spread over me. Something awful must have happened. Had she become estranged from the family? Had she become addicted to drugs? Had she disappeared? Finally, I couldn't bear it anymore and blurted out, "Do you think Andrea still remembers me?"

The answer: "I'm sure she would, honey, if she were still alive."

No. God, no. I hadn't yet adjusted to finally finding her after all those years, and now I'd already lost her again. "I'm so sorry," I stammered, as the tears spilled from my eyes.

It turns out that Andrea had been hit by a car when she was 14 years old. But that heart-wrenching phone conversation wasn't the end for us. Her mother wanted me to be part of her life—which is one of the greatest gifts I've ever received. I hadn't lost Andrea completely after all. Sabine and I continued to call each other, and a year later, I went to Seattle for the first time. That visit cemented our relationship. We see parts of Andrea in each other.

It's a wonderful feeling, six years later, to answer the phone and hear: "Hello, dear. It's Sabine."

Karina Rollins is a senior editor of The American Enterprise.

Busted

by Christine Parsons

DANVILLE, CALIFORNIA, NOVEMBER 2002: The odd squawking sound wasn't coming from my radio. It was a motorcycle cop trying to get my attention. I spotted him in the rearview mirror and felt 15 again. My cheeks flushed hot and red, as I realized that my checkered driving past had finally caught up with me.

Nowadays, teenagers are required to take both classroom and behind-the-wheel training. But in 1968, driving-instruction requirements were vague at best, leaving it to parents to figure out what to do. My mom was an overworked housewife with eight other kids to worry about—I think she saw our brief driving sessions in the family station wagon as a chance to get in a smoke before the onslaught of dinner.

"Am I making you nervous, Mom?"

She exhaled white puffs. "Of course not. Try to stay on the right side, honey."

If Mom or my two older brothers couldn't take me, I settled for my dad, whose patience extended about as far as the length of the driveway. "For Christ's sake—what the hell are you doing?!" was the closest he came to actual instruction.

How I ever passed the DMV test still baffles me.

Now the officer in the stiff leather boots tapped on my car window. I rolled it down and was greeted with, "I clocked you doing 41 in a 25, but I'll put it down as 38."

I got the feeling I was supposed to thank him. His silver, mirrored sunglasses reflected back my own tiny, pathetic image. "I can't believe this . . . it's my first ticket." The lie popped out like a bad zit right before prom.

In truth, I'd committed my first "infraction" during my junior year at the University of California, Santa Barbara. At the time I lived in a student-housing enclave that resembled a dilapidated developing-world village, and local police, understandably tired of the suntanned student activists who referred to them as "pigs," issued scads of tickets to speeding cars headed for parties, the beach, anti-establishment demonstrations, or maybe even class.

I didn't worry about traffic tickets because I got around on my bicycle in those days. But one afternoon, pedaling through a four-way stop, two uniformed officers in a parked black-and-white flashed their lights, motioning me to come over. I looked around, thinking that they meant someone else. Certainly a bike was exempt from the laws of the road . . . like a squirrel or a stray cat.

"You went right through that stop," one of the officers said. "We'll have to give you a citation."

"Uh, okay," I agreed, shoving the yellow slip of paper into my pants pocket and cycling away, making a mental note to look up the word *citation*. I was pretty sure it meant "warning."

Three months later, a couple of armed law-enforcement agents pounded on my apartment door, bearing heavy chrome handcuffs and a warrant for my arrest. The charge was "failure to appear in court for a moving violation." It took me a minute to recall the yellow paper, by now a wad of fiber caught in the lint trap of the coin-operated dryer a block away.

"Oh, that. I was on a b-bicycle. I thought it was a wa-wa-warning." I began to sob—the heaving, high-drama sobs of an adolescent English major petrified of what those policemen planned to do with those handcuffs.

"Okay, miss. Calm down. Here's a new citation. Be sure to show up this time."

So I sat in Superior Court on the appointed date, next to drunk drivers and red-light runners, waiting for the judge. "Your honor, it was just a bicycle—you know . . . pedals." I rotated my arms and hands, as if he was a foreigner who couldn't speak the language. He slapped me with the highest fine of the day.

When I went home for spring break, my dad gave me a four-speed Toyota Celica. I'd never driven a stick shift. "You'll figure it out," he reassured me with a hug as I left for school. "But for God's sake, don't burn out the clutch."

I lurched and stalled down the street, onto the highway, and all the way back to Santa Barbara. I never again got a ticket—until 20 years later, that is, when I got pulled over for weaving in my suburban-mom whale of a car. I was scanning an unfamiliar boulevard for a shoe store when my 15-year-old son changed the radio station.

The grunge-rock group Nirvana instantly sucked the positive energy right out of the car. "Mom, make him turn that off," snapped my 13-year-old daughter, thrusting for the radio buttons, inspiring a counter-grab from her brother.

I swung to break it up. Tortured cries erupted from the younger two kids, hitting each other in the backseat. My son noticed the neon red-and-blue strobe lights before I did. "Hey, Mom, I think you're getting arrested." At that point, the thought of quiet solitary confinement for the day didn't sound too bad.

I pulled over, and my driving life flashed before me, with enough illegal turns and over-the-speed-limit trips to give this cop volumes of filled ticket pads. I offered him both my wrists.

"Just your registration, ma'am," he said, peering inside the car at the kids, now so quiet that I could hear the snap-and-crackle static of his hip-mounted radio. "Did you know you were weaving?" he continued.

I shook my head and wondered what kind of food they served in prison. Whatever it was, at least I wouldn't have to cook it. "Just be careful, ma'am," he cautioned. "Okay?"

With my third infraction, I ended up in traffic school. It turned out to be a religious experience. We spilled our guts like alcoholics at a 12-step meeting: "My name is Christine. I went too fast in a residential area." I admitted my sins, did the penance, and drove away with an untarnished soul. All for a grand total of eight hours and $162.

I love this country.

Christine Parsons is a California native and mother of four.

A Conversion Story

by Jennifer Roback Morse

V ISTA, CALIFORNIA, JUNE 1996: I'm a Ph.D. in economics who started out with theories about families, theories about government, and theories about charity. Becoming a mom changed my theories. This is my conversion story.

Like many career women, my inclination was to put my kids in day care or hire a nanny. I wouldn't allow the presence of children to hinder my career advancement; in this, I'd be as much like a man as possible. In my case, it wasn't radical feminism that influenced my thinking, but rather conservative economics, with its emphasis on income-maximizing and achievement. But once my children arrived, my views changed.

You see, my particular children gave me an opportunity to participate in a continuing personal act of charity. Mind you, I didn't intend to do any such thing. I stumbled into my situation with not-so-good motives. I was a barren yuppie, fast approaching middle age, and desperate for motherhood, so my husband and I adopted a two-and-a-half-year-old boy from a Romanian orphanage. He was described as healthy, but the adoption agency actually knew little more than his name and birth date. Nevertheless, we plunged right in.

If we'd known what we were getting into, we would have been afraid to try, for Nico turned out to be developmentally delayed and emotionally disturbed. But there was no turning back for our family. And I can honestly say that in spite of the difficulties he causes, our son has changed my husband and me for the better.

As it turned out, we gave birth to a daughter six months after Nico's arrival. Anne's development has been smooth and undemanding; if we'd placed her in day care, we probably would have gotten away with it. But our son's situation didn't allow us to do this—in day care, all day every day, he wouldn't have made it. So we changed the way we live, and our daughter has benefited as well. Now I thank God every day for giving me these particular children, and for all that I've received from them.

One thing I definitely learned is that no social program could take the place of what we've done for Nico. Children must be raised one by one. There are no shortcuts that can be mass-produced by the state, "a village," or a corporation. Going from being a statistic to being our son was what saved Nico.

I also discovered that being a mother is the most important thing I'll ever do. I'd had great fantasies of changing the world with my brilliance, and it was with reluctance that I abandoned my view of myself as the center of the universe. I am, of course, the center of *my children's* universe, but messy pants and temper tantrums weren't the sort of glory I'd envisioned earlier.

Yet I learned to put one foot in front of the other, to do what has to be done even when it seems too arduous. Along the way, a message from long ago and far away became immediate and intimate: "Sell all your possessions and come follow me."

Oh, He means me! I realized. I'd always thought that message was for someone else. But it was caring for and loving these children that opened my heart to the grace of God. That grace gave me what I needed to do the seemingly impossible job.

This is why I've come to believe that bureaucratized social programs are no substitute for the giving from one person to another, which is the true meaning of *charity*. The state stands between the recipient and the donor, shielding both from the humanity of the other. The receiver becomes a problem instead of a human being in whom we might see the face of God. The giver becomes a cash dispenser, instead of a human being who might be transformed by the experience of giving.

We deceive ourselves if we think that we can reap the results of charity without the personal reality of it.

Jennifer Roback Morse is an economist at Stanford's Hoover Institution.

Teenage Angst

by Blake Hurst

WESTBORO, MISSOURI, AUGUST 1998: State Senator Sam Graves has introduced a bill in the Missouri legislature to do away with our system of annual vehicle inspections. Sam argues that less than half of the states now have these inspections, and statistics show that the accident rate in those states without them is no worse than those where inspections are still mandatory. He points out that only 2 percent of all accidents are caused by faulty equipment.

Sam is a good friend, but this time I hope his bill doesn't pass. My libertarian impulses agree with him—but, you see, I have two daughters, ages 19 and 17.

Sam's daughters, on the other hand, are eight and two. When Sam has adolescent males roaring into his driveway at all hours of the day and night to visit and, God forbid, drive off with his precious Megan or Emily, he'll begin to lose some of those libertarian urges. Now that my daughters attract multitudes of worn-out pickups steered by inexperienced drivers, I believe that inspections should be carried out *monthly*. I also favor random checks of tie-rods, seat belts, kingpins, and brake pads on each and every Saturday night.

When prom night comes for Sam in the year 2007, he'll spend a sleepless night thinking about turn signals and bald tires. (He'll also worry about other things, which is why our house groans under the weight of books on virtue, modesty, and Calvinism for dummies, required reading for all who live under my roof and eat my food.)

The first time I met my wife's parents, I was stopped in the driveway with the hood up on my car, adding oil. While I was busy visiting with her folks, at least three different vital fluids were dripping out of my old wreck. Julie's parents, always gracious, kept whatever doubts they might have had to themselves, but 20 years later, I'm not handling things nearly as well. My eldest daughter's latest beau is clean-cut and drives a new pickup, but I'm wondering if he ignores recall notices.

Whenever I read a piece in a magazine making a libertarian argument on a social issue, I'm always sure of one thing: The author has no daughters. Recently, I drove one of mine to Kansas City and waited in the parking lot while she and a friend attended a concert. As I watched several thousand adolescents stumble by my car, dropping enough aluminum beer cans in their wake to build an airliner, and using language that made me blush, my youthful flirtation with Ayn Rand was only a distant and not-so-fond memory. Personal freedom is a fine thing, but not for those who have any contact whatsoever with my two personal hostages to fortune.

Sam's bill died before the end of the last session, but an amended version, calling for inspections biannually, has passed the Senate this year and is bogged down in the House. Its final disposition is unclear, but since the state and thousands of repair shops share in $42 million of fees annually, and another $35 million is spent repairing problems found in inspections, Sam is likely to lose this session as well.

Of course, *I'm* sure to lose, too. As much as I'd like my girls to never venture away from home except to return copies of Jane Austen to the library, life doesn't work that way. It's a temptation to think that we can live apart from the world in our rural community, but that isn't possible. I guess I wouldn't have it any other way . . . but I'm not having much fun. My daughters are adults, or nearly so, and neither their mother nor I, nor any laws that the Missouri legislature can pass, can protect them from the dangers that lie ahead.

My mother, whose faith I envy, reassures me often by quoting Proverbs: "Train up a child in the way he should go, and when he is old he will not depart from it." A fine sentiment, but it really isn't *my daughters'* training that I'm worried about. If my recent parking-lot exposure to their peers is any indication, these kids aren't spending much time reading Proverbs or *The Book of Virtues*.

And my mother's faith, admirable as it is, couldn't insulate her from worries caused by my own adolescence. Within 12 months of the day the state of Missouri awarded me a driver's license, her hair turned white.

Blake Hurst is a regular contributor to The American Enterprise.

Marines for Turkey

by Suzy Ryan

OCEANSIDE, CALIFORNIA, NOVEMBER 2001: Last year I woke up on Thanksgiving morning feeling sorry for myself.

First, my extended family was celebrating the holiday in a different part of the country. Second, my husband and I had invited two Camp Pendleton Marines to join us for dinner—and I just didn't feel like cooking, cleaning, or even getting out of bed.

I didn't want to spoil the day, though. I thought that jogging a few miles would help, so I sprinted outside, hoping to end my "pity party for one." The bright sunshine encouraged me to thank God for every blessing I could think of—my family's health, food, good weather, and the like—and by the time I returned home, I felt better. But not much. I jumped in the shower as my husband and children left to pick up our guests.

About an hour later, I heard a knock on the bedroom door. It was Keegan, my nine-year-old son. "Mom," he said, "the Marines are here."

I motioned him to sit as I fixed my hair. "Tell me about them."

"They look tired, Mom," Keegan said. "They told Dad that they just finished boot camp, whatever that is. I'm glad they're here." With that, he bounded out the door.

Then it hit me: Keegan only had nine more years until he'd be venturing out on his own. Soon he might be away from his family for the holidays, depending on someone else's hospitality. Time was short, and I didn't want to waste another minute. Suddenly, the day of duty turned into a journey of joy. I was excited to get to know these two guests.

And what wonderful men they were. Throughout the day, we laughed, watched football, listened to the kids play the piano, and took a long walk. But most of all, my family and I peppered them with countless questions about their military experience. We were impressed by their willingness to serve and sacrifice for our country. We were proud to share a meal, and a nation, with them.

The day passed too quickly, and it was almost time for them to leave. "Do you guys like pumpkin pie?" I asked.

They looked at each other. "Why, yes, ma'am," Jonathan, the one from Missouri, said. "Turkey Day wouldn't be the same without pumpkin pie." I smiled and cut them each huge pieces, then watched them devour every crumb.

Soon after, we received a letter from Jonathan, who wrote, "I've been granted leave for Christmas and am very happy to get to go home. Once again, I'd like to thank you for the kindness you showed Andrew and me on Thanksgiving day. You are a good family, and a rare one at that."

But Jonathan, I should be thanking *you*. You helped me remember all that I have to be thankful for. You reminded me what a privilege it is to serve others. You changed my entire focus during the holiday season.

Enjoy your liberty passes. You deserve them.

Suzy Ryan is a writer living in the San Diego area.

DDT Lifesaver

by Joseph Jacobs

PASADENA, CALIFORNIA, OCTOBER 1998: Rachel Carson's 1962 book *Silent Spring* is the bible of today's eco-activists, even though it's unbalanced and scientifically suspect in many areas. I happen to have a personal interest in the main focus of her attack: the now-infamous insecticide DDT. You see, during World War II, as a recent recipient of a Ph.D. in chemical engineering, I was asked to develop a commercial process to manufacture a sensational, secret, microbio-logically produced germ-killer. It was called *penicillin*.

Another highly confidential product I was asked to devise a way of manufacturing in large quantities had first been invented way back in 1874. It had a long chemical name that I shortened to DDT. I wasn't told what it was to be used for—I was just given the reference to the original laboratory procedures and asked to mass-produce it in a short time. I worked diligently, culminating in a 48-hour round-the-clock stretch that successfully produced the first 500-pound batch of DDT ever made.

During that final push, a valve on one of the vessels broke, and I was covered head to foot in a two-inch coating of pure DDT, and I'm sure that I swallowed a lot of it as well. But I took off my work clothes, showered, and finished my assignment.

The next day the drums of this product I'd so laboriously produced were picked up by U.S. Army trucks. Two weeks later, Merck received a message from the Surgeon General of the Army, thanking all those who produced those 500 pounds of DDT. It had been shipped by air to Italy, where a typhus epidemic was raging among our soldiers (who were already in enough danger). Typhus is a deadly disease spread by body lice in soldiers' uniforms. DDT is absolutely lethal to body lice, so it was dusted in the GIs' uniforms, and the epidemic was stopped in its tracks. In his message, the Surgeon General estimated that 5,000 soldiers' lives were saved.

When Rachel Carson rang her alarm, did anyone try to track those thousands of U.S. soldiers who dusted their clothes with DDT and lived in daily contact with it for months to see if any developed problems? Would it have been prudent, I wonder, to refuse to use the DDT and allow those soldiers to die of typhus?

And stopping typhus is just the tip of the iceberg as far as lives saved by DDT. Before the advent of this chemical, Sri Lanka suffered 2.5 million cases of malaria a year; 25,000 of them were fatal. Using DDT to wipe out the anopheles mosquito lowered the cases to 110 in just a few years. The World Health Organization estimates that more than five million lives were saved by DDT during the first eight years of its use. Walter Ebeling, a UCLA entomologist, says that "probably no other compound, not even penicillin, has saved as many lives."

Although I'm not aware of any human fatalities at all linked to DDT, the other great chemical I'm proud to have helped bring to commercialization— penicillin—has caused quite a few deaths, from allergic reactions. Yet no one has ever bemoaned the discovery of penicillin or suggested that it be banned.

People know that there is risk in life—they face it every day. But some arrogant elitists in our society prefer not to let people make their own choices. They constantly warn us of dangers and frequently exaggerate them. Rarely, if ever, do they balance those against the benefits of "dangerous" substances. There have been enormous costs to our society as a result.

Joseph Jacobs is founder and chairman of the board of Jacobs Engineering Group.

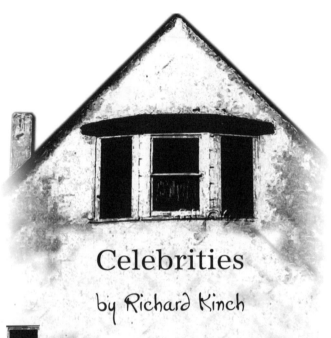

Celebrities

by Richard Kinch

LAKE WORTH, FLORIDA, APRIL 1998: Today was our first shopping adventure with our new baby, six-week-old Judy. Sallying forth into the stark reality of the local mega-mall has become our ritual of returning to the world after the confinement of pregnancy and delivery. And we've had lots of practice—Judy is our eighth child.

On this particular occasion, it seemed that everyone took notice of our family of ten: clerks, other shoppers, security guards, nervous merchants. After a while my wife, Holly, whispered nervously, "Everyone who sees us starts counting."

I know that whenever I shepherd this flock of blessings, nearly all of my vital force becomes expended in mental factoring, trying to keep inventory: eight kids; two to the third power; twice four; four pairs. Half boys, half girls, which is a nice balance. They're eight compass points, with Holly and me in the middle trying to point the way north through a stormy sea of commerce.

Some strangers will approach and speak, while others just stare. They're transfixed, because we portray in flesh and blood a life few now know. But we can't quite grasp these reactions, because we're just being ourselves.

I'd never felt self-conscious about our large family in our single-digit days—I mean, we'd often get comments, but they were always positive. Today I wondered if we were leaving quaintness behind for freakishness.

Yet after a dozen conversations with strangers, I finally came to understand that we're celebrities, not freaks. We're like movie stars—we can't go out in public without having attention focused upon us. Yet unlike movie stars, we're famous not for what we've done or pretended to be, but simply for what we are, or rather for what God has made us be.

Somehow we're able to find a few gifts for Mommy (whose birthday is two days off), smuggling them from her as best we can. I shoo everyone outdoors to the van and follow behind. My eyes linger on the leading lady, the birthday girl, the fruitful vine . . .

her hair tosses in the breeze, and the little girls about her jump and skip. My own heart is lifted. I'm joined to greatness, and the issue of that union is a blessing not just to me, but to all who are watching.

Richard Kinch is a software writer.

Happy Birthday, Pop

by Ben Stein

MALIBU, CALIFORNIA, DECEMBER 1996: Long ago, maybe in 1960 when he was running against Richard Nixon for President, John F. Kennedy was asked about some unsavory aspects of his father's life. "We all have fathers," he said, meaning that we can't be responsible for what our fathers are. But some of us have fathers whose lives are so honorable that we wish we *could* be identified with what they are. That's how I feel about my father, Herbert Stein, who just turned 80.

My father was winning things from the day he was born: declamation contests, math contests, you name it. When he was 15, he went off to Williams

College, and I think you can understand some of the main strengths of my father's makeup from three facts of his college life. First, he had a job at Williams washing dishes at a fraternity that did not admit Jews. Yet he didn't feel at all slighted and doesn't recall it bitterly; instead, he's grateful he had work to pay his way through school. Gratitude for what he has, not idle complaining and troublemaking, is one of his life's foundations.

Second, my father tried to find a job every summer that he was at Williams, and in all that time he could only find one day's work. This he *does* recall with some distress, and it also explains something about his compassionate approach to public policy. He has superb analytical ability, but he also knows that analytical ability without compassion is meager and unsatisfactory.

Third, he had the happiest day of his life just falling asleep listening to a famous game in the 1931 World Series on the radio. This shows his ability to find peace of mind through the broadcast media. They didn't have *Murder She Wrote* in those days, or my father might not have finished college. (You can't imagine how much time he spends watching TV, especially sports.)

His work life since those summers during the Great Depression has been better. I often wish that *his* father could have seen how he turned out. My grandfather used to go to brokerages during the

Depression to watch stocks move on the ticker for amusement, even though he had none. What would he have made of a son who, when he was chairman of the President's Council of Economic Advisors, could move markets with what he said? How proud he would have been—and how happy with what my pal Aram rightly calls the greatest miracle of man's existence: America.

My father is modest to the extreme. Whenever I tell him how amazed I am at what he's made of his life, he always says that this tells more about America than about him. He's never, in all the time I've known him, ever suggested any way of cutting corners or doing anything even remotely questionable. There's no amount of money that could make him say anything he doesn't believe in. I've never heard him make a racist remark—which I can also say about my mother and sister. I've never seen him make a sexist remark. And I've never seen him even look at another woman besides my mother.

Whenever a colleague questions my father's approach to an issue, his first inquiry is always whether he, my father, might be wrong, not the other guy. When he disagrees, he does it with minimum force and maximum politesse. I've never asked him for help of any kind (it's usually some arcane statistic), that he didn't furnish without a murmur, often enthusiastically. His loyalty to friends is absolute.

But even these things don't really show who my father is. You have to see him at home to know that.

You have to see him cheerfully washing dishes after dinner and singing "Drink a Highball at Nightfall" to my mother. You have to see him hold my mother's hand as they watch *Jeopardy!* night after night. After almost 60 years together, my parents are basically one person. They have a level of devotion to one another that's almost unimaginable in my generation.

You have to see my father making pancakes from scratch on a 40-year-old frying pan that his mother gave him, feeding my mother, my son, and me and explaining what Washington was like before the war, when there were streetcars. You have to see him in his apartment, puttering around with snacks, making some wise observation about the election, telling jokes, singing songs from his college days, or talking with tears in his eyes about his friends.

Richard Nixon, the Stein family's favorite President, began his memoirs by saying, "I was born in a house my father built." In many ways, I still live in a house my father built. It's a great house, filled with books and thought and love, and I feel very lucky to occupy it. And I hope to pass it on to my son.

Ben Stein is a writer, author, actor, lawyer, and a regular contributor to <u>The American Enterprise</u>. His father has since passed away.

Back from the Brink

by Daniel Janoza

CRESTWOOD, ILLINOIS, OCTOBER 1997: I never thought I'd hear the words *heroin* and *chic* mentioned in the same sentence, but lately the two have been paired in movies and other pop culture. This shakes me to my very soul, as I recall the private hell that heroin brought to my life for more than 20 years.

A single decision can determine one's life path: My seminal moment came on my 19th birthday, when a friend stopped by to help me celebrate. At the time, I'd been experimenting with all kinds of illicit drugs. Marijuana had been the first. Soon the world was a veritable candy store: alcohol, uppers, downers, psychedelics—there was a pharmaceutical cocktail for every mood. Combine this with the invincibility of youth, and life became one long party (or so it seemed). My true goal was self-anesthetization from the pain of my existence.

On my 19th birthday, however, I crossed a further threshold. For the first time, I tried heroin, and the drug became my life partner for the next two decades.

At first, there were no meetings in dark alleys or dingy bars. Drug use was easy and attractive—heroin was just another adventure. A negative experience might have been the best thing to happen on that birthday, but it didn't. Instead, I felt right at home in the sedated euphoria caused by the drug.

The insidious danger of heroin is that in early use, you're in control. You feel that you can take it or leave it; therefore, quitting holds no urgency. So year after year passed. I went to school and became a social worker. It was all right; I just needed to use responsibly. Can you believe that? A responsible heroin addict!

By age 30, the addiction was a way of life. The pain was great—an all-consuming dull throb of hopelessness and dependence that possessed my life. Greeting the day was a chore of the greatest magnitude. Sometimes I'd sleep until 5:00 P.M. because the light was too revealing. I was a creature of the night, a vampire sucking family and friends for all they were worth.

No, I didn't commit any armed robberies or burglaries, but rarely did a gift or any item of value last long, as it was sold or returned for cash. After all, what was really important? Heroin was my god. It came before parents and friends. It came before a job. It came before food and shelter. Often, it came before life itself.

Even a new faith wasn't enough to break the drug stranglehold at first. I'd expected a miraculous deliverance: God would do all the work, and I'd just sit back and wait. But that deliverance never came. It wasn't that easy—after all, recovery takes strenuous effort. A substance abuser, I learned, must make a habit out of being sober.

Eventually, with the help of God and the support of others, I was ready for that commitment . . . after decades of misery.

I've been in recovery for almost five years now, living life again. The appreciation of a beautiful sunset has returned, along with my gratitude for true love and friendship. Silly things make me laugh, and sad movies make me cry. The simple pleasures of household chores are no longer unimaginable burdens, but welcome responsibilities.

Some of my human relationships were irreparably harmed, but those who cared about me most now care again. I asked for their forgiveness, and they welcomed back the old me who was lost and nearly forgotten. I have a wife and family who never left my side, I have an emerging new journalism career, and I'm active in public service. I'll never be a literary giant or President, but I'm looking forward to the future. With God's help, I'll be the best friend, husband, father, and person I can be.

And for me, that's quite an accomplishment.

Daniel Zanoza lives in Illinois.

Living
in the Two Chinas

by Kimberly Spears

BEIJING, CHINA, MARCH 2002: Going off to China to teach English early last year was one of those "I can do anything now that I'm a college graduate" decisions that took exactly 30 seconds of intense deliberation. The sensible reservations caught up with me later.

Nervous and filled with dread, I walked into my first class at Wan Quan Elementary in Beijing. There I stood, confronted with 45 antsy eight-year-olds who all looked the same to me. I'd never been an elementary school teacher, and part of me wanted to turn around and head straight for the door. But I stayed—that morning, and the rest of the school year.

My average day required teaching three second-grade classes at Wan Quan in the morning, then shifting to Yu Ying Elementary where I conducted three afternoon classes. At Wan Quan I taught alone, struggling daily to keep my exuberant students happy, learning, and under control. Yu Ying offered me a Chinese aide, whom I accepted gratefully.

The longer I taught, the more apparent the differences between the schools became. Yu Ying had been established in the early years of the Communist party at the party's headquarters. Mao's own children had attended the school, and it became one of the premier institutions for the children of state officials. Even by American standards, the current version had many luxurious amenities, including three music studios, a dance facility, a recording suite, state-of-the-art science equipment, excess teachers, and an extremely dedicated staff.

Only three miles away from this bastion serving the offspring of the party elite, my other school— Wan Quan—seemed to exist in a different era. The children there came from working families: They arrived at school in dirty, tattered clothes and rarely had paper or more than a pencil or two. Cold and dark in the winter, uncomfortably hot in the summer, the school lacked everything from basic teaching supplies to adequate plumbing. And in the summer, it wasn't unusual for the rank smell of the toilets to permeate the air.

While my students thrived at Yu Ying, I felt stymied at Wan Quan by the increasingly difficult task of keeping a rein on the children for more than two minutes at a time. Every time I disciplined a child, it caused trauma. I made Harold cry; John spit all over my shoes when I told him to stand up; when I sent Paul to the front of the classroom, I turned around to find that he'd scribbled "SOS W.C." on the chalkboard. This eight-year-old appeal to use the restroom made me burst out laughing, which of course caused me to completely lose control of the class. These constant disruptions left me deflated and exhausted by the end of the day.

My two schools existed in different worlds, and I struggled daily to understand the disparity between them. It seemed a blatant and ironic example of the very inequity the Communists had claimed to eradicate.

I observed the same imbalance on a larger scale in Beijing city life generally. I lived on the edge of the ghetto, in the western corner of the city. There, dirt roads were littered with rotting food and discarded coal bricks, dilapidated two-room huts housed a family or more, and children played in the sewers. It wasn't unusual to see whole families living in the same one-room store in which they worked. Other than the Coke bottles and blaring TV sets, this section of town showed that little progress had been made in the past half-century or so.

Only five miles from my apartment, though, the city center thrived. Mammoth malls filled with European goods bordered Chang An Road, with its traffic jams of Volkswagen, Audi, and Mercedes vehicles. The streets were swept clean, while grass and flowers were planted everywhere. One could find the seat of government, the Monument to the People's Heroes, Mao's tomb, the luxurious Beijing Hotel, the international financial district, and about ten McDonald's restaurants. Downtown Beijing had become the perfect union of old-regime power and capitalism.

Like many in the city's emerging middle class, my students at Yu Ying have mostly left behind the oppression, poverty, and backwardness of Communist China. But only with social and political reform equal to China's economic revolution will my children from Wan Quan enjoy the laurels of freedom, too.

Kimberly Spears worked in Washington, D.C., after college.

Art of the Private

by Paul Cantor

WASHINGTON, D.C., APRIL 1996: What's an art lover to do when a feud between the President and Congress shuts down the largest complex of museums in the United States?

I had to be in Washington in November of last year, and I'd hoped to see the highly touted Winslow Homer and Johannes Vermeer exhibitions at the National Gallery of Art. But this ended up being the very moment when an epic budget showdown between Bill Clinton and Newt Gingrich left wide swaths of federal Washington shuttered for a week or more.

In recent years, my passion for going to museums has begun to border on an addiction. My friends have worried about me, especially after I reported that during a recent trip to Spain I visited 25 museums in 15 days. When you start going to places like the Museum of the Convent of the Royal Barefoot Nuns in Madrid, I suppose your loved ones do have cause for concern.

When not traveling afar, I count on the National Gallery to supply my fixes of great art. But this time, I faced a serious conflict between my political and my aesthetic principles. As a political conservative, I didn't object to the government shutdown, but that meant I had no hope of getting into the National Gallery. The thought of 21 Vermeers behind locked gates waiting to be gazed at was driving me crazy.

Then I realized that I should stop passively depending on the federal government to satisfy my craving. In all my years of going to free blockbuster exhibitions at the National Gallery, I'd been neglecting places such as the Phillips Collection. When I called its number, the recorded message proudly proclaimed: "The Phillips Collection, a non-government institution, is open today."

The Phillips turned out to be a shining example of what private initiative can do in the world of the arts. First opened in 1921 by steel heir Duncan Phillips, the institution bills itself as "the first museum of modern art in the United States." Its diverse collection is remarkably high in quality, including one of the most vivid Renoirs I've ever seen, several electric van Goghs, and one El Greco almost as good as any I saw in Spain. The American collection is a particular tribute to Phillips's taste and includes works by artists he personally patronized, such as Georgia O'Keeffe.

After visiting the Phillips, I couldn't think of any other private museum in D.C. that I hadn't already seen, so I decided to rely on the generosity of foreign governments. The Canadian embassy has a small gallery for mounting exhibitions of its country's artists. This time the embassy was featuring canvases by Cornelius Krieghoff, a 19th-century regionalist painter. Krieghoff painted quaint interiors in loving detail, although I'll be the first to admit that he's no Vermeer. Still, I relished the opportunity to see 30 of his works.

I then decided to test the spirit of hemispheric solidarity, so I set off for the Art Museum of the Americas, run by the Organization of American States. They had an exhibition of 24 recent paintings by the Japanese-Brazilian artist Tomie Ohtake, a nonrepresentational painter whose sense of color, form, and composition I found impressive.

Next, I serendipitously stumbled upon the Museum of the American Architectural Foundation in the Octagon House (where President Madison lived after the British burned the White House in the mother of all government shutdowns). This being Washington—where numbers are generally inflated—the Octagon House actually only has six sides. Yet of all the museums I visited, it proved to be the most educational. Its exhibition, "The Growth of Early Washington, D.C.: Southern City/National Ambition," chronicled a pattern of political ambition and economic overreaching that helps explain why the federal government now finds itself in financial turmoil. One display showed how, in an 1828 effort to win trade away from New York, Washington began building a canal system to Lake Erie. Having borrowed a million dollars from the federal government, the city failed to anticipate that railroads were going to replace canals, and ended up nearly bankrupt.

The public museums of Washington are a national treasure. But we shouldn't forget that those gleaming white marble buildings are monuments to the imperial ambitions of the capital city, as well as its tendency to aggrandize itself at the expense of the rest of the country. If it takes a few museum closings to teach that lesson, then, as painful as it is for me, I'll settle for Krieghoffs instead of Vermeers.

Paul Cantor is a professor of English at the University of Virginia.

Hard Rules
from Hard Times

by John Phipps

CHRISMAN, ILLINOIS, FEBRUARY 1997: For many Americans, the Great Depression lasted far beyond its official end point in 1939. Despite subsequent competition from little events like World War II, it continued to be the major formative experience for millions who grew up in its midst. Even baby boomers like me can quote glibly from Depression-era holy writ ("use it up/wear it out/make do/or do without"), because we grew up listening to ritualistic repetition of "The Lessons Learned."

In our household, these lessons boiled down to two axioms. First: "We were poor, but we were happy." This defiant statement was always followed by one or more examples of things my parents didn't have and got along just fine without. This caused me to secretly wish as a child that there could be a small period of discreet poverty for me to enjoy as well. Just some warm family evenings together with . . . well, nothing. Like the good old days.

As my sense of logic developed, I began to wonder why my parents were working so hard to acquire all those things that they knew could be gotten along without just fine. Didn't they want us to be happy— or had they discovered a way to escape being poor and still be happy? It was very confusing.

Lesson number two concerned monetary policy: "If you had a dollar, you could do anything!" This maxim took longer to grasp, as I personally have never known a period when a dollar was so difficult to obtain. In fact, for most of my life people have been trying to loan me money or send me credit cards. But for my father, the frustration of struggling to convert labor, possessions, ideas, or *anything* into cash during a contraction in the money supply was an experience not to be forgotten.

So, like the French on the Maginot Line, my parents spent the rest of their lives preparing to fight the previous economic war—and they weren't alone. I know many Midwesterners from the Depression generation who are not only well prepared for the next collapse, but who are also gingerly hopeful of a chance to put their advantage into action. Then we'll see, by George.

Thanks to the misguided Depression policy of cash starvation, a hunger for liquidity was born that has lasted a lifetime. Even modest wage-earners and businesspeople have squirreled away their money in forms as close as possible to cash. No other form of wealth gives the Depression baby such a feeling of security.

Likewise, the concept of borrowing was so darkened by moral overtones during the Depression as to require absolute secrecy when such desperate measures were deemed necessary. It's only lately that I've questioned how receiving interest could be such a righteous act, when paying it is interpreted as a sign of ignoble character.

Enter their silly children, such as me. Although not for lack of trying, the effort to transplant lessons of the Great Depression into us baby boomers has not succeeded. I understood my parents' despair on this point when I once tried to impress upon my sons what the Vietnam War was like, only to be met by blank, uncomprehending faces. Perhaps the facts can be related, but the emotions will never be shared. At any rate, my parents have clung stubbornly to their economic credo even in the face of debilitating financial storms, such as inflation. For them, the idea that cash could actually lose its value was like being sucker punched by a pastor.

The "hard times" experienced by the Depression generation produced hard rules. I suppose the economic relativism that's evident in my own life can likewise be traced back to my era. It could be that my parents' ideals will have the more lasting influence, however. My sons are devoted to their grandparents and give a weight to their words that far exceeds what they give my teachings. But then again, after my generation is through, our children may need such guidance.

John Phipps is an Illinois businessman.

The Life and Times
of Flavius

by Seth Cropsey

SANTANA, ROMANIA, FEBRUARY 2003: In 1995, I started the Adobe Foundation, which operates an orphanage for abandoned children in Santana, Romania.

Adobe opened its doors in 1998, and by March of that year I'd already done many things outside the usual career path of Washington policy wonks, such as picking up hitchhiking gypsy musicians with the intent of having them perform in the car (they did); bargaining with the city's mayor and businessmen for possession of Santana's sole remaining international

phone line; and navigating post-Communist bureau-
cracies in pursuit of a license to operate a home for
children. Now I was going to bring home the infants
to be cared for at our orphanage, Casa Adobe.

In the nearest hospital in Arad, I was escorted
by the highly capable doctor who cared for the
smallest abandoned children, as we walked from
room to room of infants in white metal beds. Half
were crying; a third were asleep; and the rest were
being fed, changed, or exhibiting what Europeans
call "hospitalismus"—head banging, rocking, and
other symptoms of prolonged institutionalization.
(Conditions have much improved in this and similar
facilities since then.)

Then I saw a little one with dark curls and brown
eyes. He was on his tummy with his head up, looking
about and—remarkably—giggling and burbling as
though he thought life was just dandy. I picked him
up, and he grinned and cooed.

"Who is this little boy?" I asked.

He was Flavius, and he was almost five months
old.

Flavius was brought to Adobe just shy of his first
birthday in October 1998. He had a curious habit the
first few days of opening his mouth and sticking his
tongue out without apparent cause. But he had a major-
league appetite, an exceptionally sunny disposition,

and his sense of humor was completely intact. He also loved music.

Adobe soon had two infants: Flavius, and a blue-gray-eyed beauty, Laura, who was one month younger. I gave the infants their bottles in the evening while seated in an old rocker listening to music. Laura liked the music and found it soothing, while Flavius turned his head toward the speakers and smiled when Bach's Goldberg variations and Beethoven's cello sonatas played. And he waved his hands around to Sousa marches.

Later, Flavius crawled up to the speakers. When he started to walk, he stood in front of them, moving his body and hands to the music. The live-in house parents taught all the children traditional Romanian folk songs—Flavius inhaled these and turned out to have a strong clear voice and good pitch (unusual in small children).

I paid one of my many visits to Casa Adobe about two months short of Flavius's fifth birthday, and I learned that he'd been picked from 27 children as one of five finalists for a music competition. I was pleased, not only for the boy, but also because this would be the first real community event in the town's recent history. Communism did not encourage a sense of community.

So one bright Sunday afternoon, I joined the crowd of parents, children, schoolteachers, administrators, businessmen, and the mayor himself in a jammed room near the center of town. There were 30 performers, ages 4 to 15. Flavius's group, the youngest, went first. All of the kids had learned their lines, but some of them were taken aback by the size of the crowd. Flavius, however, marched up to the emcee and seized the mike.

Flavius laughed, moved his body to the music, and twirled his hands during the refrain. It was a traditional song about a bunny, so he hopped, wrinkled his nose, and modulated his voice to the song's story. The audience clapped in unison, and he responded with more laughter and flashing eyes. He got a cheering ovation, and was plainly delighted by his own performance and the audience reaction.

The mayor and state orphanage director reached over and shook my hand, as I cried and laughed. But I had a dinner to attend that evening in Arad and had to leave before the judges announced their verdict. "What?" asked the state orphanage director. "You're not going to wait to see who won?"

In my heart I knew that in the most important way, Flavius had already won. And when I returned from the big city later that night, I learned that he had indeed taken first prize.

His victory convinced the town's best music teacher to accept our invitation to give music lessons to all Adobe children, while Adobe will help her as much as possible with future community events. And I'm busily planning Flavius's stage career.

Seth Cropsey is the director of international broadcasting for the U.S. government.

A Grindstone Triumph

by Blake Hurst

T ARKIO, MISSOURI, JUNE 2000: The phone rang Friday at about midnight. No parent sleeps easy once their children are old enough to drive, and a late-night phone call can make your heart stop. I restarted mine, rolled over to the nightstand, and with quite a bit of trepidation, answered the phone.

It was our daughter Ann, a sophomore at the University of Missouri, and she was in tears. She'd taken a job at the start of this semester with a chain restaurant called "Steak 'n Shake." The term *steak* here is being used rather loosely, because their steaks closely resemble hamburgers, but you do get real silverware, a waitress does come to your table, and if you stopped in Columbia, Missouri, in January, that waitress might have been Ann.

She was heartbroken, and in between sobs I managed to piece together her tale of service-industry woe. As near as I could tell, she'd made a mistake at the cash register, a co-worker had yelled at her, and her feet hurt. Not only that, but she didn't get any tables to wait on, so she was essentially working for $2.50 an hour. To top it all off, she'd had to work a half hour past the end of her shift.

A parenting crisis indeed . . . made worse by the fact that her employment at Steak 'n Shake is a direct result of some rather pointed comments by her father. Ann has been an intern for a U.S. congressman, an intern for a U.S. senator, and an intern for a statewide lobbying organization. The first two internships were unpaid, and the last paid about $4 an hour.

Her mother and I approved of these opportunities and knew that the experience and friends she made would be invaluable in her career, since she's planning to change the world within just a few years of graduation. But college is expensive, so we thought higher wages might be in order. Not only that, but Ann, over Christmas break, had given the impression that she was going to settle for nothing less than an executive position, even though we told her that the average executive-search firm isn't looking for college sophomores.

So I thought the experience of hard, demanding work would be good no matter where her career takes her, and when she writes the obligatory campaign biography, the fact that she worked her way through college waiting tables should be worth thousands of votes.

This parenting crisis should have been an easy call for me. I've spent the last ten years employing people in entry-level positions—time that I've also spent complaining about their mistakes, their unwillingness to work, and the overall decline in the work ethic. Here was my chance to strike a blow for hard work and fulfilling commitments by giving Ann a "keep your nose to the grindstone" speech. Of course, I immediately began calculating when I'd have to leave home in order to be in Columbia when Steak 'n Shake opened, so I could visit the wrath of an enraged father upon the manager, employees, and any customers who weren't tipping at least 20 percent.

When my wife, Julie, and I embarked upon this journey as parents with the birth of our first child,

I was at least vaguely aware that I'd be responsible for my children's morals, deportment, and safety. I knew I'd have to save for their education and work hard to provide for their needs. But the most difficult part of being a parent is letting go—allowing the kids to fight their own battles, make their own decisions, and grow with just the right amount of direction, but without protecting them so much that they can't deal with life on their own. Julie and I listened to Ann, encouraged her, sent her flowers, and assured her that her job would get easier.

When Ann called again, things had improved. She'd earned $30 in tips, bought a pair of comfortable shoes, and wrestled the cash register into submission. I've always been proud of all three of my children, and I was proud when Ann was selected for her job in the U.S. Senate, and I'm proud of her academic record, but I've never been as proud as that telephone call made me.

A week later, our daughter called again with the news that she'd scheduled an interview with a bank that was looking for help. She's now happily employed as a teller, and seems to be enjoying her new position a great deal. She was worried that she wasn't fulfilling her commitment to Steak 'n Shake, but an exit interview with her supervisor left little doubt that he felt her future lay somewhere, anywhere, besides the food-service industry.

I'm glad that Ann is happy in her new job, ecstatic that she's contributing to the college fund, and resigned to the fact that after countless generations of family members who earned their living working with their hands, the Hursts have finally spawned someone destined to work in a suit instead of overalls. .

Blake Hurst is a farmer and greenhouseman.

Writer-in-Hesitance

by Steve Salerno

ALLENTOWN, PENNSYLVANIA, MAY 2004: Midway through last semester, word began filtering back to the pooh-bahs at Allentown's Muhlenberg College (where I served as an adjunct professor of writing) that despite my lack of a doctoral degree, perhaps I wasn't such an unqualified disaster in the classroom after all. A horrific glitch in the registrar's computer had placed some of the English department's top students under my supervision, and apparently they were now singing the praises of their new favorite professor—yours truly. They emphasized in particular what a magnificent job I did of introducing them to "writing as it's practiced out in the real world."

Normally, this is the point where I would have been fired on the spot. But, like many liberal-arts colleges these days, Muhlenberg finds itself dealing with a sudden, inexplicable phenomenon: a surge in the number of writing students who've come to realize that not too many magazines or book publishers need trenchant works pertaining to Beowulf, or even Virginia Woolf. Students have begun demanding coursework with a more pragmatic tilt. Thus, after undertaking a broad inquiry intended to ensure that I was neither molesting the coeds nor— worse—promoting a classroom climate that tolerated sociopolitical views to the right of Che Guevara, my department chairman approached me one day. "You know, we really like you, Steve," he said. "Do you think you'd be able to teach two courses next semester instead of just one?" For this, he offered me twice my pay—the low salary of an adjunct professor.

It occurred to me that Muhlenberg's actual objective here might be to add a faculty member at wages more appropriate to jobs that require the holder to ask questions like "paper or plastic?" So a few days later, I found my way to my chairman's office. I told him that I'd be delighted to teach two classes for the school, but I wanted a visiting professorship at commensurate professorial remuneration. I assume that his laughter subsided in time.

The following day he returned, grimacing, to my dank end of the hall, to inform me that although he had no visiting professorships, the school might conceivably make me its writer-in-residence. He was careful to point out that this posed problems of some delicacy, for I wasn't exactly the prototypical author imagined in such august academic arrangements.

Colleges tend to bestow writer-in-residence appointments upon the sorts of litterateurs who are forever in danger of having the heat in their cat-laden garrets shut off or are under investigation by John Ashcroft for links to groups plotting the violent overthrow of the U.S. government. Every decade or so, they produce some impenetrable poetry or fiction for publications with names like *Zephyr of the Ephemeral Consciousness*. As part of their duties, they're expected to host semiregular public readings of their work, which, for many of them, may be the only time that work is experienced by anyone other than family members or fellow terrorist-sympathizers.

I, however, had written books people could order on Amazon, and sometimes even did. I wondered how the department could justify giving so prominent a platform to a writer whose work could be understood without the aid of mind-altering substances.

My mind swirling in such deep concerns, I asked my department chair the obvious, all-important question: "So how much would you pay me to be your writer-in-residence?"

We went back and forth on the matter of salary for several days. At week's end, the dean of faculty himself e-mailed me with the school's final offer—three times the usual adjunct rate. Or about half the rate for bona fide professors. In return for this largesse, my chairman later informed me, I'd have to "find something" to do to justify my existence.

I took the deal. After some discussion, we settled on my giving talks to local high school seniors about how writing skills can enrich one's life. I can only assume the English department sought to avoid the certain embarrassment of parading its lowly journalist-cum-writer-in-residence before more culturally aware factions, like, say, the adult population of Allentown.

But I'm not going to feel glum about such things tonight. No. Tonight I shall break out the bubbly and revel in my writer-in-residency, secure in the knowledge that that, plus the usual 50 cents, will get me a cup of coffee in the school's vending machines.

Steve Salerno writes without hesitation for The American Enterprise.

My Summer Vacation

by Mary Elizabeth Podles

BALTIMORE, MARYLAND, OCTOBER 1996: Every five years my alma mater sends a begging letter. They don't ask for money (those come every three weeks); instead, this one asks for news. "What have you been doing since we last heard from you? Fill in this blank page, which will be sent around to all your classmates." The prospect is always a little daunting. Some of us opt out altogether, while my freshman roommate once sent in Roz Chast's cartoon depicting *Bad Housekeeping* without comment.

I always need a little prodding to make the effort. Will I make a fool of myself? Will my classmates shake their heads over all that wasted potential? Will they eye me askance when they hear that I'm homeschooling my shockingly large family, and wonder if I'm the first graduate of the college to join the Vipers militia? Every time the members of some anti-government survivalist cult are arrested and their poor homeschooled children are paraded across our TV screens, a distinct frost arises in my neck of the woods, and some of the local residents gently query my friends, my neighbors, my cleaning lady, and so forth: "Are those children really all right? Are they really being properly socialized?"

Some, it's true, have stopped asking. They're the parents of the nine extra children presently in my kitchen making peanut-butter sandwiches. Perhaps these offspring have been sent over on missionary work, to help with the proper acculturation of the Podles children . . . but maybe it's something else. When my own boys recently went away to Boy Scout camp, I found that I'd inadvertently opened a small-scale boarding house, with five more children and a dog from four different families sleeping over, one of them a cousin of the family across the street who moved in with us for three days of her four-day visit. We've been known to answer the phone at dinnertime with the greeting, "Hello, Used Children's Exchange."

I've even learned a little Spanish talking on the phone with a frequent visitor's Peruvian nanny.

Some people cynically suggest I begin charging for day care. But these children have enough of that during the school year—besides, I'd never be so unsubtle. Instead, I've simply reinstated the bad old practice of conscripted child labor, and we've excavated quite a respectable pond in the backyard.

What I'd envisioned as an all-summer project was mostly dug out in a day, long before I'd even phoned away for the Lilypons catalogue. Everybody helped. True, without certain of my assistants, we probably could have done it in half the time, but it was meant as a cooperative project, and it was.

It also inadvertently turned into an impromptu science lesson. Psychologists have determined that children around the age of four ask approximately 600 questions a day. I'd add that at least half of them begin with the word *why*.

"Why do we have to level the pond's edges?"

"Because otherwise the water would spill out the low side."

"Why?"

"It's like a cup when one side is up and the other is down—water falls out."

"Why does it fall out?"

And so on. People ask me when my school lets out for summer—I'll let them know when I find out. Right now, though, I'm busy researching pond ecology and trying to calculate the proper snails-to-fish-to-plants ratio.

During my research into the mysteries of water gardening, I discovered a wonderful book written by one of the college classmates I hope not to have let down. I remember her from Mrs. Anderson's Early Renaissance Art—tall and serene, unruffled by the cruelest exam. Julie studied landscape architecture in that loveliest of cities, Kyoto, and now designs gardens so elegant and lush that I could scarcely refrain from drooling over her book. When my ship comes in, I'm going to hire her to design me a beautiful garden like a harbor, a promontory, an island, a journey of the mind . . . although I don't know how it will look swarming with all of these children.

In the meantime, I have a backyard with a pond. It doesn't look like one of Julie's archetypal landscape spaces, an image of paradise; instead, it looks a little like a hole with a mild case of drunk staggers. Someday it will be full of graceful, slow-moving Japanese carp; but for the moment, it's full of little boys planning to decorate it with frogs, tadpoles, and Lego men in very small cement overshoes.

Still the alumnae questionnaire is on my mind. "Have your children hindered your career advancement?" it asks. Certainly not. They've scuttled it forever, like the leaf boats proceeding toward the pond-sized Davy Jones's locker. Do I have any regrets?

I'm not going to say that I never look back, nor wonder where I might be now if I'd chosen otherwise. Most of my neighbors are serious professional women with interesting and fulfilling careers. Might I fit in better were I still one of them? Maybe, but I'd be missing all the fun.

And I wouldn't have a pond.

Mary Elizabeth Podles, former curator of Renaissance Art at the Walters Gallery, has degrees from Wellesley and Columbia.

the
great
outdoors

A Global Journey
Across the U.S.

by Brad Herzog

IN MIDDLE AMERICA, FEBRUARY 2005: On September 11, I was speeding through the desert toward Mecca. More accurately, it was September 11, 2002, and I was headed for Mecca, California, an isolated hamlet in the Coachella Valley populated by Latino migrant workers, barely a half hour from the oasis of Palm Springs, yet light years away. California's Mecca isn't a holy place, but this was a pilgrimage nonetheless.

To get to Mecca, I had to veer off Interstate 10 and rumble 20 miles along the rarely traveled Box Canyon

Road, flanked by jagged rock walls. There were no other cars, nor any suggestion of civilization. Ten miles in, I came upon a gravel turnoff and made an impulsive decision to pull over and inspect a sign. When I noticed the softness of the ground, and my 21-foot RV subsequently began to sink into the earth, I panicked and hit the accelerator hard, spinning my wheels deep.

Here I was, trapped in the desert, carrying a cell phone with no signal. I stood by the side of the road and waited for a miracle.

Survival had been the theme of my journey. Seven weeks earlier I'd set off in search of the fascinating and the profound. After 9/11, patriotism had swept America, but I suspected that many Americans had lost touch with much of their nation. Disregard for the country's "flyover" spaces is such a coastal and urban reflex that we've become a patchwork of stereotypes. Just look at how Hollywood portrays rural America: When Paris Hilton "roughs it" in Altus, Arkansas, a tiny community much like thousands of others that are home to a hefty percentage of our nation's population, it's like she's stranded on a deserted island: *Survivor: The Ozarks.*

America is less a melting pot than a dot-painting masterpiece, defined not by the broad strokes of national media and metropolitan muscle, but by myriad small specks that come together to form the national map. So I decided to connect some of the dots. From Paris (Kentucky) and Prague (Nebraska) to

Calcutta (West Virginia) and Congo (Ohio), I set a course for tiny communities with grand names, some of which were dwindling so fast that they may soon be historical footnotes.

My resulting book, while replete with zany encounters with nudists and hermits, hippies and Hare Krishnas, is primarily about people struggling to survive in America's nooks and crannies: for example, the ranchers in the blink-and-it's-gone Oregon hamlet of Rome (population 29) fighting to save their land from what they consider environmental zealots; the black treasurer of Cairo, Illinois, working to salvage a city nearly destroyed by racial unrest a generation ago; and the wife of an MIA Navy pilot from the Arizona copper-mining town of Bagdad whose husband was shot down over Laos 32 years ago. She still clings to the hope that someday there will be a knock on her door, and he'll be there, gray-haired and home.

Meanwhile, back in Mecca, an elementary school principal explained the difficulties of educating migrants' children, many of whom work in the fields themselves and don't attend class until well into the school year. But a local high school teacher *was* named National Teacher of the Year in 2002. Former Army colonel Chauncy Veatch was flown to Washington with two of his outstanding students. After being called a hero at a White House ceremony, he pointed to his students and said, "Well, I'd like you to meet *my* heroes." Which is how migrant-worker children found themselves applauded by the President of the United States.

Yes, I made it to Mecca. But as I stood beside my sunken vehicle, I wasn't sure I'd make it out. There I was, a Jew stuck in the desert. A 40-year wait seemed plausible.

Irony arrived in a rented sedan. Some Germans— Stefan and Claudia, taking a whimsical ride through Box Canyon as part of their three-week vacation through America's West—transported me to a service station, where I phoned for a tow truck.

I waited a few hours at a joint called "Leon's Other Place," where I got some food and read the local paper (the English version). A brown-skinned man in the booth next to me was eating a sandwich and reading the paper, too. "F---in' al-Qaeda," he muttered.

The tow-truck driver appeared. He was Latino, born and raised quite near Mecca. A sticker on his windshield read, "And the flag was still there." I offered a handshake. "Hello, I'm Brad."

"Hi," he replied, "I'm Israel."

There's a sermon in there somewhere.

Brad Herzog is the author of Small World: A Microcosmic Journey.

Fishing
for Life and Death

by William Vande Kopple

TIPPY DAM, MICHIGAN, MAY 2000: Each autumn I take a little trip that makes my friends wonder about my judgment. In the late afternoon, I head north to the Manistee River below Tippy Dam. By the time I arrive, the sun has almost set, and the walkway down to the river—where the king salmon are spawning— is being blotted out in darkness. I start fishing at dusk and continue through much of the night.

First I stash my spare tackle on the bank, then I light my lantern and balance it on some rocks. Next

in real life

82

I start looking for a good place to wade into the river. It's after I hook a big fish that I face problems with footing. Many of the bigger kings, especially if they're fresh from Lake Michigan, make runs hundreds of yards downstream from the angler. If you have a reel that holds that much line, you can try to keep your place in the currents while the fish bores away toward the big lake. Then once it tires, you hope that you'll be able to pump it back upstream to your net.

Reels that can store that much line, however, are too heavy for me to hold throughout the night. So after any fish I hook charges off about 75 yards from me, I have to start chasing it or it will pull all the line off my spool. Staggering downstream in strong currents with only wavering streaks of light from lanterns on the shore to guide me isn't exactly the safest thing I do in life.

More than once I've swung a foot into the side of a rock and lurched desperately to keep water from spilling over the top of my waders. My most dangerous chase took me near an old birch that had been blown into the river, its branches throbbing against the current. I had no way of knowing that two men fishing downstream from that birch had tied a stringer to one of its outermost branches, and on it they'd secured seven or eight kings. The fish were lying resignedly in a little pool below the branch when I tried to plant a boot across several of their backs. I assume they weren't too happy about having the nylon cord of the stringer threaded through their gills, and I *know* they weren't pleased to have my boot stomped among them.

These fish weigh about 20 pounds, all muscle, and their sudden thrashing tossed me off balance. I was able to arrest my fall, but I jammed my knee against the sharp edge of a rock. For months afterward I carried an uncomfortable but iconic reminder of my misstep—water on that knee.

Since a stumble that fills your waders can drown you, it doesn't really make sense that what I fear most while fishing at night isn't a fall, but rather the backcasts of other fishermen. One of the attractions of fishing at night is that the river isn't as crowded with other anglers, but some congregating in certain spots is inevitable.

Imagine several guys standing near each other, whipping ten-foot rods to get the momentum for long casts. The sound of rods and lines snapping in the air is eerily entrancing. But if fishermen don't check the spaces behind them, they can easily drive a sharp hook into a fellow angler's flesh. What a flashing hook can do to parts of the human body is, without exception, ugly.

So far I've never been hooked. The closest I came was when a guy took my cap off. A little *whup,* some rustling of my hair, and my hat disappeared into the dark. His string of apologies made it more difficult for me to forget how narrowly I'd skirted the pain.

I've seen three fishermen with hooks in their bodies. One had a treble hook of a Mepps spinner in the well-defined muscles of his left arm. The hook entered the man's forearm and bore a neat arc through the muscle, with the barb emerging about a half-inch lower on his arm. The victim took out his pliers, cut the barb off, grabbed the hook by its shank, and wiggled it backward out of his arm.

Another guy wasn't as fortunate, since he'd been hooked just above the collar of his wool shirt. The point and barb had penetrated the muscle of his neck and stayed there, so one of his friends had to try a different method of extraction—he bent the eye of the hook down toward his friend's neck, then took some of his heaviest fishing line and looped it under that curve. He wrapped the ends of the line around several fingers of his right hand and gave the line a sharp yank. He tore up the tissue on his friend's neck a bit, but the hook pulled out, giving off just the slightest slurping sound.

A third victim needed assistance that he trusted no one at the dam to provide. He had the hook of a half-ounce Little Cleo spoon in his nose, about half an inch up the left side. The barb hadn't emerged from his flesh, and everyone could see that the curves of his nose and cheek allowed no good angle for a fishing-line yank. So after glancing skeptically at nearby anglers who were pulling rusty jackknives and bloodstained tweezers out of pockets in their vests, this man decided to drive 20 miles to the clinic in Manistee. As he packed up his gear and headed up the bank, the lure, hanging down along the side of his mouth, fulfilled the promise of its nickname: "Wigl."

Even in the face of such actual or potential troubles, I'm going to continue to make these excursions. Why? Well, ultimately it has to do with mystery, struggle, and revelation.

When a king salmon strikes my lure at night, a battle starts that leaves my forearms cramping, the small of my back aching, and my feet knocking into rocks and pieces of driftwood around me. I never get to see what's fighting me on the end of the line until I haul it up on the gravel of the shoreline. Then, using a small flashlight's beam to cut narrowly through the dark, I gaze at what I've wrested from the dark and swirling swiftness—its eyes intent on the spawn, glinting with knowledge of life in death and death in life. I suck breath sharply past my teeth. It is clearly a thing of beauty.

William Vande Kopple teaches English at Calvin College.

Race of a Lifetime

by Karl Zinsmeister

RIVERS AND LAKES OF THE U.S. AND IRELAND, AUGUST 1996: In the neon world of sport, rowing is a softly glowing candle. It offers little glamor for participants, and hardly any rewards at all to spectators. Yet from my first moments of taking up the sport as a college freshman, rowing had me in its grip.

I started as a football player at Yale and tried rowing as a lark, but I immediately switched teams when I found how much I enjoyed competing on the water. My freshman crew ended up being the first in recent memory to beat Harvard (rowing's superpower). That earned us a 3,000-mile trip to the sport's mecca—the

Henley Royal Regatta in England. My sophomore year I ended up in the heavyweight varsity boat, and that July I again journeyed to Henley.

Somewhere in the course of that sophomore year, a shift in the relative positions of my academic and athletic lives took place. I never liked the cultural and social scene at Yale, and it took me a couple of years to find the right direction in my academic work. Early on, it was rowing that saved me. Our dawn and evening practices were pure adventure, and my successes an unexpected gift. Every day on the water brought new possibilities.

But once I made the transformation from striving novice to established member of a top crew engaged in the sometimes grim job of winning a national championship (we did), rowing lost a measure of its joy. I began to feel ground down, caught in a giant machine. Almost simultaneously, I began to pull together the threads of my academic career. I laid out an exciting research project that would bring me to Dublin's Trinity College for all of my junior year, and then back to the National Library of Ireland the following summer to write a thesis of which I could be proud. One fever waxed as another waned, and I set off permanently down the path toward a life of the mind.

Rowing was the last thing I was thinking about as I stepped into Trinity's historic courtyard to attend my first class in Dublin. But as I was tripping along the waxy cobblestones, I suddenly had company. The stroke of the Trinity rowing team, Jerry Macken, recognized me from my races at Henley, and instantly began to recruit me—hard. As I listened to his sweet Irish brogue, I thought, *Man, this guy could sell vacation homes in Lebanon.* By the time I'd crossed the wide courtyard I found myself telling him, like a lost adolescent encountering his first Hare Krishna in a bus station, that, okay, maybe I *would* row a little bit with them.

The Trinity Boat Club was just what its name implied—a student-run club, where everything from boat maintenance to fund-raising was handled by the rowers themselves. And notwithstanding its epic stature in the works of James Joyce, the Liffey is a narrow, tortured snake of a river. In places it's little more than a stream, thick with marshy grasses and dangerously protective mother swans. Racing 60-foot-long shells on such a watercourse was often a hair-raising adventure.

The contrast with the Yale crew—where we had professional riggers as well as coaches, large motor launches, indoor circulating rowing tanks, dozens of eight-oared boats, a training trip to Florida when the ice froze, buses, food service, and straight rivers— was, shall we say, sharp. But I was impressed by the ad hoc energy of my Irish teammates, and thoroughly won over by their hilarity and warmth. As our season progressed, a powerful momentum began to build. Our final four weeks of racing turned out to be some of the most exciting days of my athletic life.

One of our volunteer coaches that year once compared getting a boat to "swing," as oarsmen say, to eight men trying to throw a single javelin. He might have said that it was like eight men trying to throw a single javelin while effectively blindfolded, under the direction of a ninth, non-exerting person—the coxswain.

My own attempt to describe what's necessary for good rowing would be something like this: At medium power and speed, rowing is pure rhythm and fluidity; eight hearts beating in time. But at full tilt, it's as if some quirky aeronautical engineer had invented a human-powered helicopter which, given sufficiently frantic efforts by an octet of bulky men, was occasionally capable of short bursts of wild, careering, high-speed flight—just along the treetops—yet subject to an instantaneous crash given the slightest letup.

Flight is not easily achieved, but it provides unspeakable exhilaration when it is. By the end of my year in Ireland, we were flying regularly. We were very, very fast, and we were going to Henley.

When the team arrived in England, I learned something interesting: My old Yale comrades had also had a fine season, and in pursuit of the world's most famous regatta medal, they too had journeyed to Henley. It made for a dramatic surprise meeting from across the ocean.

For Trinity, our long year of difficult training capped by the brilliant June workouts stood us well. We won our first three Henley races easily and made it to Sunday, Henley's final day. And our opponent was . . . Yale.

It wasn't until then that I took stock of my position. When I'd escaped Yale the previous summer, I could never have guessed that at the end of the following season I'd be facing old teammates, coaches, and memories (both sour and dear) from a seat in a crew occupying an opposing lane. It was a bittersweet, almost shocking little trick of fate that had brought together these two poles of my life.

Yale's Henley entry that year had crushed all of its American competition. Pale and comparatively undersized, our Irish crew must have seemed improbable behemoth-slayers. But I knew in the most intimate way possible—namely, months of communal life in both camps—that there was little difference in talent between our teams. And surprise would be on our side. Never before had I felt so flushed before a race.

Surprise was indeed ours. In what I still remember as one of the most sublime half minutes of my life, the Trinity team rocketed off the start and took nearly a length lead. It was the only time Yale had been behind another crew that entire year.

We were careering. We were way above the tree-tops. Our coxswain was screaming for us to pass their bowsprit, but our relative positions seemed to freeze. Like two great stags with intermeshed antlers, the two teams were locked. We stayed that way for a mile—five agonizing minutes.

As we approached the public enclosure, I'm told there was an avalanche of primal noise from the huge crowd. Yale began to creep closer. I felt as if my temples were flexing, fibrillating to the alternate pressures of blood from the inside and sound without. They were drawing within a few seats. Our stroke rating was in the clouds. Some later claimed that there was a choppy stroke in the mix—I have no recollection.

There is a mountain of hyperbolic melodrama attached to sport today. But I tell you this: When that race was finished, I was paralyzed. I didn't know who won, nor would I for several minutes. My first concern at that moment was to regain control of my body, clear my head, and force down the hysteria I felt choking me. I was afraid to swallow for fear I'd gag. Every milliliter of oxygen was precious.

As I slumped—gasping, drooling, knees locked—I listened to Jerry Macken suffering in front of me. We drifted. It was very quiet. Then it came to me: that beautiful, floodlit, musical race. We'd lost! The lead changed hands on the last stroke. Our times, by human standards, were identical.

After we put the boat away for the last time, I realized how little I'd understood what was happening to me during the course of that year. I spent the final minutes of my season of "taking a break" from rowing . . . sobbing violently into a towel.

The American Enterprise editor-in-chief Karl Zins-meister won national championships in college rowing in both the U.S. and Ireland in the 1980s.

My Cherry Red

by Blake Hurst

TARKIO, MISSOURI, AUGUST 2001: It's red, with lots of chrome. It's so tall that I had to spend $250 to have a step installed so that I could climb into the cab. It has six gears and a 240-horsepower Cummins diesel engine that will pull a 24-foot trailer at 80 miles an hour for more than 400 miles without stopping. I know that because I've traversed Nebraska on I-80 with my new behemoth, which is not an experience for the weak-kneed.

(For those of you who think that I drive a little fast, understand that on the plains of Nebraska, you do 80 or get run over.) The CD player has better sound than any home system we own, and I find myself playing it as loud as any 16-year-old with a boom box. I am, of course, a little embarrassed by all this, but I must admit that my new Dodge pickup truck has brought me a great deal of pleasure.

The new truck replaced an old Dodge with 190,000 miles, a torn front seat, a front bumper held on with baling wire, and no radio at all. I kept the old pickup for two reasons: (1) It's still mechanically sound, and (2) my wife, Julie, won't let me drive the new one over our farm.

A week or two into harvest, I had to admit that she had a point. I hit a particularly nasty bump when trying to balance a cup of coffee and my cell phone while dodging shrapnel from the seat and dash. Thermoses were flying, a biography of John Marshall that I'd borrowed from my brother two years ago and still haven't finished was sliding to the floor, at least three days of newspapers were fluttering in the breeze, and I had a particularly nasty scrape with a flying crescent wrench.

At the same time, I was coughing and sneezing because during soybean harvest everything is coated with a thick layer of bean dust, which, as a result of my bouncing, was becoming airborne in a noxious cloud. It's not a fault of mine to be overly careful with my possessions, at least until the "new" wears off, so I want to avoid this kind of abuse of my latest purchase. After all, it cost more than the profits from my first two years of farming.

Still, my pickup has experienced the bumps and bruises of everyday life here on Hurst Farms. Once, years ago, we had a tarp installed on a grain truck. The fellow who put the tarp on used a picture of our vehicle in his advertising for years. I had more than one neighbor comment that he'd done so because "everybody knew" that, to coin a phrase, if it could make it on the Hurst Farms, it could make it anywhere.

This time, within a week of bringing my new pickup home, Julie came running into the house, announcing in the portentous tones that only wives are capable of that we had a problem, and I'd better come quickly. The new truck had been parked outside my office the previous evening, with its plant-hauling trailer attached, but when I came around the corner that morning, it was gone. It wasn't hard to find, though—you could track it by the huge plume of highly flammable propane gas boiling up at the end of the driveway. The truck had rolled the length of a football field, collided with a thousand-gallon tank of propane, knocked the tank off its moorings, and severed the copper line that attached the tank to the greenhouse heater it supplied. Gas was spewing, my new truck had lost its virginity, and it was all rather tense until the valve to the gas was shut off.

Fourteen-year-old boys are not noted for hiding their emotions, so it was easy to discover the cause of the roaming Dodge as soon as I saw Ben's face. Like all boys his age, my son felt that he's ready to drive, so he'd been doing a little practicing with my new pickup, shifting gears while no doubt supplying motor noises and imagining adolescent girls wilting in his wake. But he neglected to set the brake at the end of his session. A lesson well learned—we can't get in a vehicle now without releasing the parking brake, because Ben spends his evenings setting the brakes on each of our cars and trucks.

I am a conservative in every sense of the word, and I know that man shouldn't be a slave to his possessions, that material things matter little in the long run, and that the kind of vehicle one drives has absolutely no correlation to a life well lived. I grew up working with a grandfather who never threw *anything* away. I spent weeks straightening used nails, and once devoted a few days to recycling some barbed wire so rotten with age that it broke at the touch. I asked Grandpa how old it was, and he said he didn't know, because it was secondhand when he built the fence in 1931. So this sinful pride in my ostentatious conveyance is decidedly out of character.

But I'm getting ready to leave for a trip to a neighboring town, and I admit that I'm going to enjoy hearing that diesel rattle while Merle Haggard wails, and I survey my domain from the seat of my cherry-red pickup.

Blake Hurst never drives 80 outside of Nebraska.

The Gift of Life

by Robert Cheeks

EAST LIVERPOOL, OHIO, FEBRUARY 2004: In the 1950s, my family lived amid a mix of Irish, Italian, English, German, Jewish, Greek, and Ukrainian families. It was a decidedly working-class neighborhood that provided a labor pool for the local potteries, steel mills, and associated businesses of the upper Ohio Valley.

My favorite pal among the horde of children in the locale was Bruce "Smitty" Smith. We hit it off right away as five-year-olds. Smitty was the kid who got straight A's without any significant exertion, understood fractions, read all the Hardy Boys mysteries, and was talented with his hands.

While I spastically smeared glue on my scale models of Sherman tanks and Nazi fighter planes, he was altering the plastic bodies of his car kits to make the doors swing open and the steering wheel turn. Bruce laid out a scale model of the Pittsburgh Pirates' Forbes Field in the basement of his house—complete with a carved wooden bat that pivoted on the floor thanks to rubber bands and springs. There were baselines, a painted infield and outfield, and bricks representing infielders and baskets standing in for outfielders. All you needed was a marble and you were in business for hours.

St. Aloysius Catholic Church and School was the center of our little universe. We were altar boys, choir boys, and Boy Scouts. We usually got stuck serving at the funerals because the older kids took the weddings (which inevitably resulted in a tip from the best man). I didn't mind, though, because the local funeral director, Frank Dawson, always had a joke to tell or some sage advice to offer on the way to the cemetery.

My favorite time of year was Advent, when on Friday afternoons the different grades would pack the stairwells of our school and sing Christmas hymns. If the nuns and priests at St. Aloysius taught us anything—and they taught us a great many things—

it was just how precious life is. Some of us, however, had to learn that lesson the hard way.

It was in February of 1956 when Smitty and I found ourselves bundled for the single-digit weather and sledding on the Seventh Street hill. After four or five trips down the speedy run, we rested near the small stream known locally as "Stink Creek." There had been a thaw the previous week, resulting in a rather impressive flood along the flats adjoining the creek, and when the weather turned cold, the entire expanse froze in crystalline majesty.

I trekked out on the ice and stamped my foot. "Solid as a rock," I pronounced. Just then there was a loud crack, and the ice parted. I was instantly engulfed in an unimaginable terror. As I fell through, I managed a "Jesus, Mary, and Joseph"—and then everything turned milky gray.

Weighed down as I was with a winter coat, scarf, hat with earflaps, two pairs of pants, woolen mittens, and buckled calf-length rubber boots, I should have dropped right to the bottom of the creek. But the current was so swift that instead of descending I darted downstream . . . under the ice!

As I rose I struck solid ice. I opened my eyes and looked into the murky water all around me. As I rose again I thrust upward, and my head struck ice again. This time, fortunately, I broke through. My depleted lungs sucked in great volumes of sweet air.

At just that critical moment, a large tree limb slapped down in front of my face. It was Smitty. When I hadn't surfaced, he'd followed along the bank of the creek, picking up a fallen tree limb as he went, and when I finally burst through the ice, he was there with his life pole. After a great deal of exertion, he pulled me out of the water and across the ice to the shore.

Ten-year-old Bruce Edward Daniel Smith had saved my life with his quick thinking, stalwart determination, and courage. Yet all I could say was, "Thanks, Smitty."

"Yeah," he replied, "it's okay."

Neither of us said much after that as we walked home.

I've always hoped that someday I might repay my old friend. But there are some debts that simply can't be repaid.

Robert Cheeks is from Ohio and writes frequently on American life.

Gone to the Dogs

by Christine Parsons

DANVILLE, CALIFORNIA, FEBRUARY 2002: Getting the dog was Michelle's idea. She's the youngest of our three daughters, and the only bleeding-heart tree hugger in our otherwise conservative family. When she first developed her canine obsession a few years ago at age nine, my husband and I encouraged her to purchase every volume on dogs that the local Barnes & Noble offered. We figured that a roomful of books on pups could substitute for the real thing. Then one day she let slip to Dr. Berman that she knew all about dogs.

Dr. Berman is the Mister Rogers of local pediatricians—he wears funky sweaters and has a soft twang like Fred. *"Tell me,* Michelle," he asked, drawing his words out long and slow as he tapped her right knee with his reflex hammer, "what dogs do you know about?"

"Which group?" Michelle asked, swallowing hard and clearing her throat. "I mean, there's the sporting dogs, hounds, working dogs, terriers, toys, non-sporting dogs, herding dogs . . ."

Dr. Berman glanced over his shoulder at me, ever so pleased with the direction the conversation was taking. "Wow. You know, I have a dog myself. He's a springer spaniel."

"Sporting dog," she said, smiling from one dimpled cheek to the other.

Dr. Berman/Rogers gave me a wink and a nod, and I left "The Neighborhood" with an unspoken understanding that the canine expert should have a dog.

Michelle spent weeks poring over her copy of *The Complete Dog Book* by the American Kennel Club in search of the right breed for a family with an allergic dad and an apathetic mom. Some sort of self-motivated, non-shedding dog was what we needed. She finally came to us with the picture of a border terrier.

"Isn't he cute?" It had the face of an otter and the body of a large rat.

A neighbor who owned the same type of dog gave me the name of a breeder on the East Coast who might have one we could adopt. The breeder, Mary Beth, did have a dog available but was reluctant to let it go to just anyone. The animal was already traumatized from a previous placement where there were other dogs in the house who were hard to get along with.

"She's a bitch," said Mary Beth.

I thought for a moment. The last thing I needed was a dog with an attitude. "I don't know, Mary Beth," I said. "We already have a couple of those in the house, if you know what I mean."

She sighed. "Oh, then this may not work. This bitch needs to be top dog, which is why she came back to us from her first owner. They had three other bitches, and it was a mess."

Oh. *That* kind of bitch.

My total lack of canine knowledge had Mary Beth worried. She began to ramble on about how a dog is a huge responsibility that isn't for everyone. To sidetrack her thoughts I changed the subject to food. What kind did she recommend for the . . . uh . . . bitch?

"A dog is just like a person," she explained, echoing a Michelle-ism. "It needs good nutrition."

I stared at the open box of Oreo O's cereal inches from the phone and nodded. "That's so true," I responded.

Mary Beth promised that if—a big *if*—*we* were accepted as the dog's new owners, she'd send me her recipe for Quick Canine Hash, a blend of whole-wheat couscous, beef chuck, and bone meal. I vowed to buy the freshest ground beef around, keep her dog safe from the pool, walk her every day, and anything else I could think of to get the pup into my daughter's hands.

Mary Beth hesitated. "These dogs rarely come back. I may just keep her. Kizzy's special."

"So is Michelle. She *needs* . . . what did you call her?"

"Her name is Kismet."

Kismet. The flesh on my arms tingled and I felt a wave of nausea. It was an Oprah moment. Could it be that I—a hard-hearted, gas-guzzling, watt-blowing Republican—was *meant* to have a warm fuzzy animal in my life?

"Your neighbor told me about Michelle," said Mary Beth, interrupting my thoughts. "I think she'll be good for Kizzy." She agreed to send Kismet via United Airlines, and I told Michelle the news when she got home from school.

"Can't we get her *today?* And what the heck is a kismet, anyway?"

"It's something that was meant to be . . . fate." I made a mental note to pick up a large bag of very dry dog food—hold the meat—at the supermarket.

Several weeks later we loaded the Suburban with Michelle's three cousins, a dog leash, plastic bags for poop, rags in case the dog threw up, and my sister, Joni, who already had a dog and would be the voice of reassurance.

"Geez, what if this dog is like . . . *Cujo* . . . remember that horror movie?" She snarled, and we both laughed. But what if the dog *was* monstrous? Should we leave it and run? Was Mary Beth chuckling back in Massachusetts, thrilled to rid herself of the b-word?

We parked curbside. The kids raced ahead, crowding around the pick-up counter. And then Michelle dropped to her knees to peek inside a beige dog kennel. A pair of dark chocolate eyes met her blue ones.

"Oh, Mom, look at her. She *does* look like a Kismet."

She was petite and quiet and shaking all over. We put the leash on and took her out for a walk as the last of the evening's jets roared overhead. I kept thinking how strange life was, with a dog coming to us all the way from the other side of the country. It *did* seem to be . . . fate.

Kismet and I get along fine in spite of our opposing political philosophies. True to her liberal roots, she thinks she's entitled to *everything:* food, shelter, medical care, even walks along the Iron Horse Trail.

Luckily she can't hear me listening to Rush Limbaugh on my headset radio as we stroll.

But it's Michelle who gives her all that gooey stuff like smooches and cuddles and a warm spot on her bed every night (the left side, of course). I peeked in on them recently, and the realization hit: Democrats—give them an inch and before you know it, the whole house has gone to the dogs.

At-home mother of four Christine Parsons is writing a book about bringing back the family dinner.

Selling the Universe

by Michael Casper

ITHACA, NEW YORK, DECEMBER 1998: A little more than two years ago, I was looking through a magazine when I saw a small ad that offered meteorites for sale (yes, meteorites . . . space rocks . . . cosmic debris . . . the rarest material on this planet). It had never crossed my mind that a regular person could own a meteorite. I sent away for a catalog, placed an order, and was hooked.

I've always collected unusual things, and soon I had an awful lot of meteorites. My wife, Cathi, and I had just sold our espresso café, so we were trying to figure out our next step. As my meteorite collection took over more and more of the house, we decided to see if we could turn this passion into a business. Through lots of hard work, we've grown to where we're now one of the largest meteorite dealers in the world, with thousands of clients in every corner of the globe.

There are three main classes of meteorites: stones, irons, and stony-irons (also called *pallasites*). Stone meteorites are those with exteriors most similar to terrestrial rocks: When sliced open, they can be found to contain flecks of metal or spherical bodies called *chondrules*. Irons are meteorites whose composition is primarily that mineral, with small amounts of nickel and cobalt—it's extremely dense and heavy in proportion to its size.

Pallasites are meteorites made up of both stone and iron, and many of them contain beautiful olivine crystals that can be seen after they're sliced. Within these three main classes there are literally dozens of subclasses, and our inventory has representatives of nearly every type, including a small lunar specimen and meteorites from Mars. We have gigantic irons that weigh several hundred pounds, as well as delicate and beautiful pallasites.

While this may sound glamorous, it's a lot of hard work. I travel more than 80,000 miles annually by truck, going to shows and buying specimens, while Cathi handles the administrative side of the business and the shipping. We rarely work less than 14-hour days. My two sons, Ariel and Gideon, ages ten and eight, go to several shows a year with us. They help with security, along with loading and unloading the truck with more than a ton of meteorites. Gideon even has an area in our booth where he sells minerals. Our phone starts ringing before breakfast seven days a week and often goes well into the night, with calls from all over the world. And we answer an average of 50 e-mails and faxes daily.

Meteorites are referred to as either "falls" or "finds." A fall is just that—a witnessed entry where the meteorite is hunted down shortly thereafter. A find is a stone stumbled upon and later identified as a meteorite.

Meteorites have names—they're named for the postal location nearest to where they were seen or found—and they're priced by weight, with the more plentiful irons ranging from five cents per gram (for really large and heavy specimens) to $10 to $15 per gram for rare irons. Stone meteorites can be priced anywhere from $1.25 per gram to hundreds, sometimes thousands, of dollars per gram for those that are extremely unusual. A few pallasites, but not many, are priced under $20 per gram.

Who collects meteorites? Everyone. Our customers range from the most prestigious museums of the world to the 12-year-old boy in California who saves his allowance and calls us twice a year. We have clients who are serious collectors and others who buy the rocks simply because they're fascinated by the idea that they can own material not of our planet. Our customers also include scientists who study meteorites in an effort to unlock the mysteries of the universe. One group of stone meteorites called *carbonaceous chondrites* contains amino acids—so does the human body. Food for thought?

We get our meteorites from contacts around the globe. In the Sahara Desert and the Antarctic, meteorites are readily visible to the naked eye, and hunters of the rocks risk their lives traveling to these locations and others to scour the land. Potential risks are great, but so are the rewards. Sometimes we buy from other dealers, but we also exchange meteorite material with many of the world's major museums and educational institutions.

In addition, we receive dozens of rock samples a week from individuals who believe that they've found a meteorite. Many people think that meteorites contain colors like red, blue, green, or yellow, and that they glitter (neither of which is true). Meteorites don't have any kind of predictable appearance, other than an exterior that appears "burnt." Iron specimens often contain indentations that look like thumbprints.

Many meteorites have been uncovered by farmers while plowing; others have been found using metal detectors (99.9 percent of all meteorites will attract a magnet, if only slightly); and some discoverers just notice a strange rock and are persistent in their identification attempts. Meteorites can be found anywhere by anyone. Anybody going searching would do well to arm himself with a powerful magnet, a metal detector, and some luck.

So the next time you're outdoors on a crisp night and you see a shooting star, remember that you're watching a piece of another world go dancing by. What secrets does it contain? Where has it been traveling for the last several million years? Will it reach the surface of our planet? And what will it tell us if it does?

Michael Casper built his meteorite business into the largest trader of space objects in the world.

Roundup

by Hendrik Mills

HARLEM, MONTANA, FEBRUARY 1998: What would you call a day of hard toil on someone else's farm for no pay? You're getting your pants covered with wet manure and being kicked by hoofed animals, and when you're suddenly thrown on your rear end in the mud, your "co-workers" laugh insensitively and make crude jokes at your expense. And all you receive in return is a meal after the danger is over.

Are you being exploited? Perhaps you should pursue a legal claim against the person who's created this "hostile work environment." Or you could stop whining and enjoy being one of the lucky few who get to be part of that great western tradition: cattle branding!

Ranchers brand their cattle for the same reason your car has a serial number. And the day on the Kulbecks' ranch begins with a ragtag group of mounted cowboys, volunteers on foot (like me), and the owner of the spread trying to surround the cows and calves that are scattered over a large pasture. There may be several hours' delay, as we had this May when a few dozen cows decided to swim across the Milk River rather than be herded into the waiting corrals.

Nevertheless, the bovines are eventually bunched up under some cottonwoods. We then shoo each animal, one at a time, through a metal gate into the system of pens. Once inside, this mooing, alarmed, and overcrowded bunch has to be separated. Some have horns, all have hard hooves and more heft than I do, and they mill around chaotically.

The new calves are the ones we need to brand, and to do this we must temporarily separate them from their mothers, wrestle them down, and apply the hot iron—without being trampled by the mothers in the process. The superiority of brain over brawn is clearly demonstrated when about 1,200 pounds' worth of men and boys wade in and succeed in separating about 20,000 pounds of frightened calves from about 90,000 pounds of upset mothers.

Three or four men will single out a cow, surround it, and simultaneously wave their arms and shout, leaving a gap for the animal to rush through. This gap leads, of course, to the corral we want it to enter, and the gate is opened just in time and then slammed shut after the animal rushes past. When this fast-moving entertainment is over, the branding takes place.

We ready the inoculation needles and heat up the branding irons (each Kulbeck brother has his own). Certain participants will serve in teams of two as calf-wrestlers—I'm one of them. One of the Kulbeck grandsons, age 11, will open and close the gate of the calf pen, so only one animal at a time can come into the branding area. Two cowboy ropers, a teenager and an elderly man, will take turns dragging the calves out of the pen one by one. The elite positions of inoculator and brander are reserved for the Kulbeck brothers, Tim and Charlie, themselves.

A horse-mounted roper rides into the pen, twirling a loop. He deftly lays the rope down on the ground just in front of some calf's rear leg. If the calf steps in the lariat, he jerks it up, closing the rope around the animal's rear leg. Then he rides slowly out of the pen, pulling the calf out with him.

As soon as the calf clears the gate into the main corral, my partner and I run up and each grab a flailing leg. We yank upward suddenly, and the animal finds itself lying in the dirt on its side with the wind knocked out of it—consequently, we have about three seconds to position ourselves to hold it down before it regains its bearings. The "head man" kneels on the animal's neck and holds the calf's upper front leg in a bent-double position, while the "tail man" sits on his rump on the ground and immobilizes the calf's rear quarters by grasping them tightly with his legs and arms. I get this job.

The calf now has three of its four legs in an awkward and constrained position, so it can't get away—we hope. Tim calmly applies the red-hot branding iron to the exposed flank of the calf, about 6 inches from my leg and 18 inches from my face. The animal bawls and thrashes, but Tim methodically rocks the hot iron back and forth so as to make a readable and permanent brand. I'm not stout, and it's all I can do to keep hold of that kicking rear leg with both hands. My incentive is the knowledge that if the leg gets loose, my face will be the nearest solid object for it to contact. A thick cloud of smoke, generated by that branding iron as it ignites hair and skin, billows around my head. A rancher 20 miles north once told us that he couldn't brand his bison calves because when he tried it, they caught on fire. I believe it.

Charlie injects some vaccine, and we're done. At the count of three, both calf-wrestlers let go and spring up and away from the animal. Since castration was done by the tight-rubber-band method at birth, the male brandees are spared the slicing that I saw at another branding. (When castration does occur during branding, it may be followed later by a "Rocky Mountain Oyster Fry," often a big social occasion.)

With three teams of wrestlers, we branded 85 to 90 calves. It didn't all go smoothly: A calf that wasn't tackled soon enough by the wrestlers ran wildly in a circle with the roper's horse as a pivot. Tim Kulbeck was standing unawares, branding iron in hand, in the path of the taut rope and was suddenly sent sprawling forward. Fortunately, he didn't brand himself.

When all the calves were marked and the tools were put away, the calves and mothers were reunited and it was mealtime. Julie Kulbeck had produced an impressive spread of food, with which we capped off a satisfying day. I made sure to compliment the plentiful food and drink. You see, I don't want to be left out when branding time comes around next year.

Hendrik Mills teaches school when he's not wrestling calves.

Soul on Ice

by Mayer Schiller

MONSEY, NEW YORK, APRIL 1998: As a rabbi, I teach Talmud daily in a yeshiva. My outlook is decidedly apocalyptic, because I think our civilization's supposed defenders lack the fortitude these grim times require. But there's one thing I'm never gloomy about: sports—hockey, football, and soccer. Mostly hockey.

Camus once wrote that he was never at peace off the soccer field (strange peace—he was a goalie!). I know what he meant, though: No matter what else is up or down in my life, sports is always up. Watching. Playing. Coaching. Officiating.

Since 1979 I've been involved with the Metropolitan Yeshiva High School Hockey League in various capacities. Currently I serve as commissioner; however, from 1991 to 1995, I coached my school team to five consecutive championships. Oh, I've also lost my share . . . and they were heartbreakers, too. We lost the '86 championship in sudden death after we'd tied it up with 12 seconds to go. And we lost in 1980 in the semifinals against a fourth-place, below-.500 team.

I've celebrated with teams that have captured championships in dramatic fashion, and life doesn't have many sweeter moments. And I've been in losing locker rooms surrounded by wonderful young men, and those moments are special, too.

But it's not just about winning or losing. I draw deep solace from the "tremendous trifles" of the game: The stats. The rules. The sound of the puck hitting the boards, of the referee's whistle. Game days become enchanted.

Sports, especially physical ones, are a refuge from many of the sicknesses of the modern world. They demand courage and masculine camaraderie. They're essentially romantic, in the deepest sense of the term, in that they create quests and beckon us to pursue them. Ruthless capitalism has harmed professional sports, but on the local level, especially in private schools or community leagues, these distortions are kept away, and sports remain just that: sports.

Several years ago, I was coaching a team that wasn't given much of a chance of winning the championship. After each practice, when one of that squad's members would drop me off at my home, I'd ask him, "So, David, are you going to be a champ?"

David was very far from being a "champ" in his schoolwork, and he'd just lived through his parents' messy divorce. His inevitable reply was, "I sure hope so, Rabbi, I sure hope so."

Well, we did win that championship. And on the night of the final game, when David dropped me off after the celebration, I turned to him and said, "Well, I guess you *are* a champ." He just nodded, kind of teary-eyed.

About five minutes after I walked in the door, the telephone rang. It was David, and in a voice choked with tears he asked, "Rabbi, am I really a champ?"

"Yes, you are. Forever."

"Thanks, Rabbi. I just wanted to hear you say that again."

Western civilization may be doomed. But moments like that make God's world infinitely sweet.

Rabbi Mayer Schiller teaches Talmud at the Yeshiva University High School.

The Guy Has a Gun

by Ray Wisher

GULF COAST, FLORIDA, JUNE 1998: It was no big deal; just another night on patrol. My partner and I were in an unmarked car driving in a residential area late at night when we saw an SUV speed by and run a stop sign. The back window was also open, as if somebody had just stuffed something into it. We began to follow the truck, passing by as it turned down a dead-end street and pulled into a driveway a few blocks down. To make sure things were okay, we drove down to the cul-de-sac to make sure that the owner belonged there.

As we slowly cruised by, I looked to my right and saw, to my horror, a young white male with long hair running toward me out of the shadows—and he had a small semiautomatic handgun in his right hand. The look on his face was wide-eyed rage. I watched as he approached my side of the car at a dead run, reaching over with his left hand to pull back the slide on the firearm.

"The guy has a gun!" I yelled. Yet I couldn't do anything but watch as the man ran within 20 feet and pointed the weapon at my head. I told myself that there was no way this guy had a real gun. *Nobody's that stupid,* I thought. *It must be some kind of pellet gun or something.* I watched as the man, still running, stuck the gun at me and pulled the trigger three times. And I heard *click, click, click.*

Thinking that he must be trying to scare us, I said, "It must be a pellet gun." Luckily, my partner slammed the accelerator to the floor and skidded into the cul-del-sac so that we could end up facing the assailant. He hit the blue lights as we bailed out of the car, guns pulled. We yelled for the man to drop his weapon, and as soon as he saw the lights he dropped the gun and threw up his hands: "I didn't know you were cops!" he exclaimed. "I'm sorry."

Still thinking that it had to be some kind of pellet pistol, I walked up and asked why he was trying to scare us like that. He said he thought that he was being followed, but he wouldn't tell us why someone would be following him.

I picked up the pistol and looked at it—to my surprise it was a .38. Then I pulled the slide back, half expecting to find it empty. Nobody would actually try to shoot someone they didn't know just because they were driving down the road in a car. But the gun wasn't empty; it was fully loaded. Seeing that the first round had jammed down, I ran the slide back twice. A round ejected nicely from the port. My blood ran cold.

That the gun hadn't gone off was sheer luck—or God's hand. Because the man hadn't pulled the slide back far enough to feed the bullet into the chamber, the round had stuck. Before the bullet I ejected hit the ground, I looked at my partner and said, "Cuff him."

The man had no real criminal history, wasn't insane, wasn't on drugs, and wasn't drunk. He had no reason for what he did. "I didn't know you were cops," he repeated. I told him that wasn't a good excuse: "What if we'd been just some old lady, or a couple of people lost and trying to find an address?" I asked him. "You can't just run out and start waving guns around."

What an idiot, I thought as I hefted the blue steel pistol in one hand and the hollow-point bullets in the other. Then the reality of what almost happened settled in—*what a pair of lucky cops.*

Police detective Ray Wisher is a frequent contributor to The American Enterprise.

Running
from Men to Man

by Naomi Riley

NEW YORK, NEW YORK, NOVEMBER 2001: I was a slow child. My gym teacher once congratulated me for completing a 15-minute mile, and I can't think of a childhood torment I dreaded more than running. It was, therefore, with some surprise and not a little trepidation that I found myself at the starting line for the New York City Marathon last November.

As I moved through the crowd of tens of thousands, I remember wondering yet again how I'd come to think this would be a good idea. It had been New Year's Eve, and the combination of champagne, confetti, and the threat that New York might be hit by terrorists at any minute probably clouded my thinking. A few of my friends, with much greater athletic prowess than I had, had already decided to run. I also figured that it would be a good way to get my mind off of men. It sounded like the perfect feminist antidote—sweating away the memories of college sweethearts and disastrous blind dates. I was a modern woman trying to make it in the big city, looking to the future, soaring to new . . . well, you get the picture.

So, the first Monday morning of the new year, with the throngs of other Upper West Siders working to remove the evidence of holiday gorging from their thighs, I hit the gym. I should disclose that I wasn't starting from scratch—since moving to New York I'd been running about three miles several times a week. So the question became, *How do you get from 3 to 26.2 in 11 months?*

Friends who'd run distances before insisted that there's a hump right around the four-mile mark—but then your breathing regulates, and you stop feeling like you're going to collapse at any moment. It's difficult to fathom that your fifth mile will be easier than your second, but it's true. By the end of May, I was able to do a five-mile loop in Central Park, take a walking break, then run some more.

In late spring, prospective New York City Marathon runners have to make a commitment, at least a financial one. There are several ways you can enter the marathon: If you've proven that you're fast enough in another official marathon, you automatically get in; otherwise, you have to try the lottery. New York City admits about 29,000 people, while several thousand more apply. Until last year, to enter the lottery you either sent in an application by mail or e-mail, or you'd come to Central Park on a Sunday morning with thousands of other people and stand in line for hours. A much higher percentage of the entrants were taken from the people who came in person, so I stood in line—and I got a place. (This year, the lottery was conducted entirely over the Internet, with the first few entrants picked ceremonially by the mayor.)

Over the next month or so, I upped my distance until I could run for almost two hours, with one or two walking breaks. People who don't run, or those used to running short distances for exercise, find it hard to imagine how anyone can stay interested in something so mindless for hours on end. In fact, one of the biggest obstacles to marathon training is boredom. I run with a Walkman (the test for any song is whether, no matter how winded you are, you occasionally find yourself singing it out loud). Some of my friends, though, wouldn't dream of wearing headphones. They use their running time to write entire articles in their heads, figure out how to dump their girlfriends, plan their week's wardrobe, or just think big thoughts.

My mind wanders while running, too, but the music is there when I need inspiration. Often, though, the best inspiration is another person. Unfortunately, by the beginning of July—when the weather was steamy, the distractions plentiful, and the time for serious distance running had arrived—my friends from the New Year's Eve party had given up. Things looked pretty bleak even though my training schedule was as follows: From the end of July to the middle of October, I was to do a long run every other weekend, increasing the distance by 2 miles each time, so that by three weeks before the marathon I would have completed runs of 10, 12, 14, 16, and 18 miles. All of these runs during the summer months had to be started by 8:30 A.M. or earlier; otherwise, the heat became overwhelming.

Facing this regimen without the encouragement of company, I suddenly didn't feel like one of those strong, determined women in the sneaker commercials—I was tired, bored, and hot. Then, on a Friday night at the end of July, I found myself on a date with an acquaintance who'd run the marathon a couple of years before. When I told him that my friends had dropped out, he said that I simply could not quit, and that if I needed company for my longer runs, he'd be happy to fill in. Eight hours after he put me into a cab in Greenwich Village, he appeared on my doorstep in running clothes.

My summer loops around the park went a lot faster after that. Then, finally, I was standing at the starting line in Staten Island. I sailed across the Verrazano-Narrows Bridge, which shook from the weight of all the runners. I ran through the streets of Brooklyn, where the crowds were so loud I couldn't hear my own panting. At mile seven, I saw the smiling face of my training partner, along with my mother's camera pointed at me. The adrenaline pumped pretty steadily all the way to mile 14—when I decided to eat one of my PowerBars while walking over the first half of the 59th Street Bridge.

My cousins and some friends were in the crowd on the other side. (You have to tell everyone ahead of time on which side of the street you plan to run so they can find you.) The miles in northern Manhattan and the Bronx can be pretty discouraging: The crowds thin, and you realize that even though you've run 18 miles, you're nowhere near finished.

Finally, about five hours after the start of the race, I entered Central Park. I turned up my music and picked up the pace. When I came around the last corner at Columbus Circle, I could see the finish line. I felt nauseated . . . until I thought about the people waiting for me at the other end, one guy in particular. I wanted to laugh when I remembered why I started all this, but I hardly had the strength to smile.

No sooner had I completed my post-race pizza than my companion suggested that we run the marathon together next year. Delirious, perhaps, I agreed. Still, I can't say that I wasn't a little relieved when I found out recently that I didn't make the lottery. This year, *I'll* wait for *him* at the finish line.

Naomi Riley is a regular author for <u>The American Enterprise</u> who eventually married her running companion.

Taps

by David Broome

ARLINGTON, VIRGINIA, MAY 1996: The time is 4 A.M. There's no light as I walk out into the cold predawn air. At 04:15 hours, a staff sergeant screams, "Fall in!" and two dozen scattered troops suddenly coalesce into three neat columns, standing perfectly still with rifle in hand, prepared for the morning's inspection.

Stopping in front of each troop, the sergeants slam their feet together with a terrific crack of the metal plates on their shoes. Occasionally they inform some individual that he must fall out of the formation and repair the inadequate parts of his uniform. Every man wonders, *Did I shave closely enough? Is there a piece of lint on my uniform—even a tiny thread hanging from a button or seam?* Fortunately, the darkness may conceal small blemishes.

Once the sergeant passes me without complaint, my heartbeat slows to its normal rate. I'm ready for duty with other members of the presidential honor guards posted at Arlington National Cemetery. Today the U.S. Vice President and the President of Hungary will lay a wreath at the Tomb of the Unknown Soldier, with all four military services and the Coast Guard representing their uniforms.

After a short bus ride, the platoons assemble in rank and file from tallest to smallest. The Army, in charge of all joint-service ceremonies, is fortunate to be led by one Sergeant Major Massey. His booming voice unifies all the soldiers, sailors, Marines, and airmen into one machine. As the sun dawns, he barks in my ear, "Rock steady, young honor guard soldier! Show 'em who the superpower is."

Now assembled at the base of the tomb, I wait impatiently to hear the thundering rounds from the howitzers at the bottom of the hill, which will announce the beginning of the ceremony. Standing motionless, already on public display, I observe out of the corner of my eye the amusingly frantic sniffing of the Secret Service dogs.

All at once I jump, nearly losing my military bearing as the first howitzer round bellows through the still cemetery. I feel the percussion as my pant legs vibrate against my knees. The hoarse voice of the sergeant major calls out: "Army and Marine platoons, for-ward march!" Then I hear the measured tap of the shoes as the first platoons march up to post on the tomb. Next comes the call for Navy and Air Force platoons.

With all five platoons marking time, the commanding officer orders a halt. He's a 6'2" Army colonel in his ceremonial blues. I look in amazement at the decorations covering the broad expanse of his chest. He comes to a slow, robotlike halt before slamming his heels and raising his sword to salute the tomb and the sacrifice it represents. Saber in hand, he calls the honor guard to attention before the dignitaries, guests, and tourists.

The VIPs come forward, and the colonel calls the honor guard to present arms. As I snap my M-1 to the center of my body, my cold palms sting from the slap of the wooden riflestock. After the wreath is placed, the band plays an unfamiliar anthem to honor the Hungarian leader, followed by the "Star-Spangled Banner." Hats come off, hands cover hearts, and the pathos of sorrow mixed with pride swells in my heart.

When the song ends, a lone bugler steps forward to play "Taps." A deafening stillness blankets all, as thoughts of the supreme sacrifice previous men have given for their country remind the soldiers of the seriousness of their duty today. Then leaders take charge of their platoons, and we march away in rhythmic cadence. The ride back to base is quieter than usual.

David Broome is a former member of the Air Force Honor Guard, and now serves in the Reserves' 459th Security Police Squadron.

Hunting for Manhood

by Ray Wisher

CAPE CORAL, FLORIDA, DECEMBER 2001: Brett's a good boy. But he lives in a confusing and tempting world of sick music, bad morals, poor schools, and rampant drugs. And like many 14-year-olds, he was unfocused, rebellious, and trying to figure out life when I met him through our church.

As a police detective, I know how easily kids can get lost. And I knew that Brett's friends were an assortment of teens with criminal records, blue hair, and baggy jeans. So one day last winter I resolved that this boy wasn't going to become one of them. I decided to introduce him to something that would get his attention, make him work, and challenge him to discipline himself. I took him bow hunting.

The deal was simple: *Do better in school, respect your parents, and think more about the future.* In return, I'd take him into the woods to stalk wild pigs. Brett couldn't wait to get going.

First I set up a bag target and showed Brett the basics of how to aim and shoot an arrow. He was sticking arrows dead center from the outset. We held contests, and he often beat me. He became pretty sure of himself. Then I made him run and do push-ups to create the adrenaline dump that often leads to poor shooting during an actual hunt—his overconfidence faded as the arrows began bouncing off the ground and sailing clear of the target.

After a few weeks, I felt that he was ready to try some field scouting. That night a big boar slipped into the thicket where we were set up. I was crouched behind Brett as the pig started rooting only 15 yards away. Brett slowly turned his head, and all I could see behind his camouflaged face were two huge eyes. His breath was ragged, and he seemed to be grinning from ear to ear. When the boar finally figured out we were there, he began to circle us instead of running, once getting within ten feet as he tried to stick his snout into the blind.

Brett was hooked. He doubled his efforts on the practice field. He shot standing, from his knees, in the open, and behind cover. He began reading bow-hunting articles, trying to understand the best techniques. His mother called to thank me, saying that his grades were coming up. Over and over, I drilled him on the ethics of our sport—on the honor involved in doing it right.

One evening we went to the woods and climbed two skinny pines in the middle of a thicket. Shortly before dark, I heard sounds from our left. I watched as Brett quietly pulled back his bow and aimed. The arrow struck, and the pig wheeled and took off. It was almost dark when we started tracking, and I was disappointed that there was no blood. We'd traveled about 30 yards when there came a low rumble from the thicket in front of us. We backed out, and soon the rest of the pig's group surrounded us, growling, grunting, and snapping teeth. Brett was excited beyond words. He'd shot his first pig, and now we were in a standoff with rooters.

Two hours later, exhausted and frustrated, we had to call it a night. We'd grid-searched the entire area and found neither the pig nor a trail. I explained to Brett that part of bow hunting is the fact that there are no guarantees. He was heartbroken, yet I could see that he understood what all ethical hunters know: the seriousness of taking an animal's life without its successful recovery.

A few weeks later we tried again. When the pigs came crashing through the palmettos, Brett got ready. A spotted pig rounded the corner, and Brett pulled back and aimed. He waited for it to turn broadside, as he'd been taught, then released. The pig took off with the arrow sticking out its other side. We got down and started to track. After a few yards, I found the bent arrow and large amounts of blood nearby—this one wasn't getting away. Indeed, we soon found the pig, dead as a stone.

Brett jumped around like he was on fire, and he yelled the same yell every young hunter has yelled since the beginning of time: He was a bow hunter! No bad grades, poor schools, or family troubles could take that from him. I made him drag his trophy back to the truck, where he called his mom and dad on my cell phone.

Time will tell about Brett. But I know that he now has a grounding in something that could lead him to a more disciplined way of life. The boy is a hunter. And that means something.

Ray Wisher is a police detective who hunts in Florida and Alabama.

Softball Dynasty

by Blake Hurst

TARKIO, MISSOURI, OCTOBER 1997: The catcher is 60 and has a heart condition. She's also my mother. The first baseman is 61 and has lost a step. And let's face it: Dad didn't have a step to lose.

They've hidden me in right field. One summer, when I was 16, I played on a baseball team with ten players. It was awfully lonely in the dugout while everybody else was out in the field. I don't think we won a game all summer, and it's a little hard to accept that you're the worst player on the worst team in the league.

After two knee surgeries, my wife plays intermittently. She was the only family member who could run well, and now it's painful for her (and me) when she runs at all. My two brothers play shortstop and left field. One of my sisters-in-law plays second base—she's the best hitter on the team, but four pregnancies have robbed her of her speed. She has an unorthodox fielding style, stopping all ground balls with her shins, and then throwing the runner out. My youngest brother recently married, and his wife now plays catcher ever since Mom started having chest pains. The third generation rides the bench, although a couple of them are excellent athletes. But as long as I'm paying for their Nikes and car insurance, I'm starting.

My family fields this team in two coed softball tournaments every summer, and if it isn't clear by now, we aren't very good. Coed softball is slow-pitch, played with five men and five women per team. The men and women must alternate in the batting order, and if a man walks, the woman following him in the batting order also walks. Two walks thus result in a run scored and the bases loaded, so your pitcher must have good control. This fact has caused some family difficulties. Dad was our first pitcher, and he had a little trouble with his control. In fact, we lost our first several games by an average margin of 20 runs. It's tough to put your father on the waiver wire . . . so I let my brother do it.

But we have a wonderful time. It's easy to forget, when you read about player strikes and their latest antics, that sport is supposed to be fun. Here in northwest Missouri, where most of our sports news comes out of Nebraska, there's a popular joke. Question: When you see two Nebraska football players riding in the backseat of a car, who's driving? Answer: The sheriff. But sport as practiced by our family is simply for fun. Although we try very hard, the thrill of victory and the agony of defeat are both rather muted.

We're no strangers to a more physical kind of agony, however. Team members have had two pulled hamstrings, two broken bones, cartilage tears, and more sore muscles and strawberries from sliding than you can count. (It's a truly sublime sight to see a 250-pound farmer attempting to slide into second base.) Tournaments sometimes last until well past midnight. By the fifth or sixth game of the day, muscles are stiffening, and the will to win is burning less brightly. By the seventh or eighth game, the second loss in a double-elimination tournament is akin to the end of World War I. We don't really care who won—we're just glad it's over.

All my aches and pains have healed, but I still remember the catch I made seven years ago on a deep fly ball hit to right field. This selective memory is endemic to all who participate in sports, and no doubt explains why many professional players hang around long after they should leave. All of us have forgotten how bad we look in short pants, and we're quick to overlook the plays we can no longer make. Instead, we're making plans for next year's tournament. One of us is on the 270-day disabled list due to pregnancy, and our pitcher has signed a free-agent contract with a bank in another town and will have to be replaced. But we're optimistic about our chances. In fact, this year we may even practice.

Blake Hurst, who still hates to sit on the bench, is better than the average right fielder.

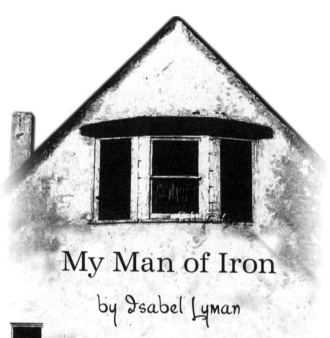

My Man of Iron

by Isabel Lyman

KAILUA-KONA, HAWAII, SEPTEMBER 2003: "I was wondering how my body was going to do it from the ten-mile mark of the run onward. But during the last quarter mile of the marathon, the crowd was loud and supportive. I've never had so many people cheer for me." So stated my 45-year-old husband, Wid, in the land of manta rays and muumuus, after facing the super-sized challenge of the Ironman competition.

This world championship for triathletes requires participants to swim 2.4 miles in the choppy Pacific Ocean, bike 112 miles across windy lava fields, and then run 26.2 miles in the heat and humidity. And the race must be finished within 17 hours.

Wid was joined in his quest by 1,540 athletes between the ages of 19 and 80 from around the world and 49 states. Ironman officials report that more than 100,000 gallons of fluid replacement and 600 bottles of sunscreen were used up during the grueling race. More than 7,000 enthusiastic volunteers lining the 140.6-mile racecourse did the dispensing and cheering.

Wid finished in just under 15 hours. As he jubilantly crossed the finish line in downtown Kona, I hung a lei of tropical flowers around his neck, and our 17-year-old son, who was working security for the event, embraced him with a bear hug. My hubby was now an official man of iron.

The course proved to be as intimidating as advertised. "Every stage was harder than I thought it was going to be," Wid said. But somehow he successfully completed this race, which provides the very definition of "survival of the fittest."

More than 20,000 triathletes vied to compete in the Hawaii Ironman this year. Most competitors qualified by placing in one of the 23 Ironman races held throughout the world. A lucky 150 gained entrance via a lottery that gives amateur athletes an opportunity to participate with the pros. Wid won one of these lottery slots, then had to complete a half-Ironman race to validate his entry.

Kent Laird, a 29-year-old webmaster from Beaverton, Oregon, also won a lottery slot. I asked him, a former college runner and father of two young children, why he voluntarily submitted himself to this madness. Laird's explanation seemed to be the universal one: "I've wanted to do the Ironman since I was 13 or 14, after seeing it on television a long time ago. This is 'the event.' I'm drawn to things that test your body and mind, and that let you see what you can do on a given day."

Don't try this at home, kids. My athletic husband prepared for Kona for four years. Several months before the actual race, he increased the duration and intensity of his workouts. He swam 8 miles, biked 250 miles, and ran 30 to 35 miles each week. It was even tougher mentally than physically. Wid often got through the long hours of training by praying and listening to taped Christian music. Call it the power of iron prayer.

While he did most of his training in Massachusetts, where we live, Wid spent a month in Oklahoma City to acclimate to the hot and windy conditions that prevail there as in Hawaii. Not until race week, however, did he actually swim in the ocean.

"It was hard to stay on course because of the currents, and other swimmers kept getting in my way," he said of the long dip. The choppy seas caused several triathletes to drop out with seasickness. But winds, ocean, and even triathletes who stopped along the bike course to retch didn't stop Wid. And he finished the race with renewed respect for the professional triathletes like that year's Ironman champion, Tim DeBoom of the United States, who completed the race in 08:29:56.

Wid has no plans to return to Kona next year. He came, he raced, he conquered. It's time now to be a little more laid back, to "Live Aloha," as they say in Hawaii. *Mahalo* (thank you), says his wife.

Isabel Lyman assumes that she is now a First Lady of Iron.

One Move
and I'll Shoot

by Gaye Wagner

SAN DIEGO, CALIFORNIA, FEBRUARY 1995: With enough
time logged on the streets, all of us police officers
can remember a time when we lost, or almost lost,
control. I remember chasing a speeding black Camaro
years ago through busy traffic, with lights, siren,
and adrenaline blasting. I was alone, and unable to
transmit the location or plate number because of
heavy radio traffic. The driver unwittingly yielded
a mile down the road because he thought I was en
route to an emergency call.

The Camaro was low to the ground and black throughout, and the windows were heavily tinted. The driver was black and decked in black Harley-Davidson garb with chains hanging from his belt. I had trouble seeing into the car, and my instincts told me to beware. I asked him to step out—he did, but he kept his right hand from view. On the sidewalk, I asked to see his hands. He ignored me, keeping his right side away from me. I repeated my request; he ignored me. When I raised my voice in command, he turned and fled into oncoming traffic. As he turned, I saw silver in his right hand and believed he had a gun. Like a dog chases a cat, I went after him, yelling into my radio as I did.

We ran along the street's yellow divider and in and out of traffic. Some vehicles swerved to avoid us, while others pulled over. The suspect ran down a side street, then into an isolated canyon area. I lost sight of him briefly, but then I closed in enough to draw my gun. I yelled for him to raise his hands and drop to his knees. He turned, and I yelled commands with my eyes fixed on my sights. He dropped to his knees, but still I couldn't see his right hand. I shrieked for him to lie flat on his stomach, arms spread in front. He fell on his stomach with his right hand under his body.

My heart and lungs were exploding from the run and the anticipation that he had a weapon and would turn on me and fire. My training told me to hold him at gunpoint until cover arrived and he could be safely handcuffed. My brain told me that I was going to shoot this man unless I could cuff him and know his hands were secured and I was safe. I walked up, put my pistol to his head and, with words that surprised me, said, "One move and I'll shoot your ass."

By then he clearly believed that I was a crazed woman who would in fact pull the trigger. I had him slowly move his hands around to be cuffed, then left him prone in the sand while I recovered, choking from runner's cough.

When some cover officers finally ran up, I patted the suspect down. When I didn't find a gun, I asked him why he'd run. He answered, "Because I didn't have a license."

By now I was starting to come down; my brain had moved from primal cruise control to almost-human comprehension. "What? You ran for no license? A third of the people on the road in California have no license." Still coughing and weak from the run and the expectation of my first gunfight, all I could think was, *I almost shot this man for no license?*

Suddenly I was furious at his stupid behavior. I started screaming that he could have gotten us both killed. I swung my foot to kick him, but my cover officer grabbed my arm and pulled me aside.

As it turned out, there was more to the story. The driver was no sweetheart: He was a career criminal and drug offender on parole who was high from speedballing. The Camaro he drove was stolen, with a stolen engine from a second car, and license and VIN plates from other cars.

All in all, it was an ordinary occurrence in this job. But this took place not long after the Rodney King incident, and it made me ask myself: *Could I have been one of those officers under the microscope?*

Gaye Wagner was a patrol officer with the San Diego Police Department, then a detective.

Frogs

by William Vande Kopple

MYERS LAKE, MICHIGAN, JUNE 2001: A few years after my third son was born, I bought three pairs of rubber boots, some nearly unbreakable fiberglass fishing rods, and some dependable reels. Jon was seven; Joel, six; and Jason, three, when we set out on their first fishing trip.

I had high hopes. But as we walked to the lake shore, a leopard frog jumped across Jason's path. It was the first of dozens, all basking in the sun among the grass. When we came trundling through, they burst into a popcorn frenzy of jumping—many into the water, some away from us, and a few actually bouncing off our legs.

The boys took several quick looks—at me, at one another, and at the frogs. Then, simultaneously, they dropped their rods, yanked off their boots and socks, and started creeping and lunging after the frogs. When one would catch a prize, he'd bring it over to show it off. "Look, Dad, look!" he'd exult, as the nearly squished frog excreted orangish liquid through his fingers and down his forearm. "It's a great big one, maybe the king of all the frogs, but leaking like crazy!"

The boys weren't happy when after 40 minutes or so I marched them back to the car, the greenish residue of goose droppings on their knees, blades of grass between their toes.

"But I thought we came here to fish," Jon said.

"I thought so, too. But we can't now," I replied. "When you guys tossed your rods on the ground, you got the lines all tangled up, and there's sand in the reels—if we use them now, we'll wreck the gears." They sulked for a while, but on the way home it took them only a couple of miles before they started bickering about who'd caught the most frogs, the largest frog, the fastest frog, the rarest frog, the most colorful frog, and on and on.

"How did it go?" my wife asked, as I carried the mass of rods into the basement.

"It was a mess," I sighed. "We never even got a line in the water. We walked into jumping frogs near the shore, and all the boys wanted to do was chase them."

"But when they came in, they were really excited . . . it sounded like they had a great time."

"It was chaos. And now I have half a day's work trying to untangle the lines and clean out the reels. I don't think I'll take all three of them fishing at the same time ever again."

About a dozen years after this fiasco, Jason and I were resting on the south bank of the Au Sable River after dark. He and his brothers had become fine fishermen (instructed one at a time!), and we were waiting for the wonder of the hex hatch to start. The crickets and peepers were clamoring, and every 30 seconds or so a bullfrog would belch out such an alarming croak that we'd jump a little.

"That last one must be the king of all bullfrogs," Jason whispered.

"I guess."

"Dad?"

"Yeah?"

"Do you remember that day you took us out to that beach to hunt frogs?"

"Huh?"

"You weren't the best frog catcher, and all the time you had goose crap smeared on your cheek. But that was a mad-awesome day. Do you remember it?"

"Hmm."

"Do you?"

"I'm afraid it's coming back to me."

William Vande Kopple, a professor, has nothing against amphibians in principle.

Harvest Time

by Blake Hurst

TARKIO, MISSOURI, FEBRUARY 1995: Weather. Perhaps bond traders mark their lives by bull and bear markets, real-estate agents by their last big sale, baseball players by balls and strikes, but here in the rural Midwest, we remember weather. I can't recall my first date with my wife, my high school graduation, or anything I learned in college, but I *can* remember the weather from every year of my life here on the farm. Julie and I were married in a drought year; our first child came home from the hospital after an ice storm; and our second daughter was born after a three-inch rain that saved our corn crop—perhaps the only instance where labor has been induced by successful pollination (of corn).

Last year the weather was a disaster: 24 inches of rain in July flooded our bottom ground and ruined the crops on our hill ground. But this year we're enjoying harvest because our weather has been wonderful. For years, one of the seed companies ran a television commercial that had a smiling farmer on his combine exclaim: "Man, that is real corn!" The commercial would have been more realistic if the guy had had a three-day growth of beard, a skinned knuckle from a recalcitrant nut, and clothes that looked a little less like those from an L. L. Bean catalog, but the ad did a good job of capturing the feeling that comes with a good crop.

Of course, harvest, even in a good year, is not always a great deal of fun. We work seven days a week, 14 hours a day, unless we're combining soybeans and the dew doesn't arrive early. If the beans stay dry, we'll run from 7 A.M. until 2 A.M. That's a long day.

And harvest is accompanied by its share of frustration. In our first week of harvest this year, the transmission in one of our trucks breathed its last; I spent two days suspended 30 feet in the air trying to repair a grain bin; we had flat tires, and escaped cows, and combines broken down, and . . . well, you get the picture. The price of corn is low, the cost of repairs is high, and we have another six weeks of this to look forward to.

Here on the Hurst farm, harvest is a family affair. We have two combines, three trucks, two augers, an auger wagon, four farmers, three farmers' wives, a fiancé, five pickups, and seven grandkids. All this must be moved from farm to farm over a large part of Atchison County as we bring in our agricultural output. An invasion of Haiti takes less logistical skill than planning out a typical day here in the fall. We communicate with commercial band radios and cellular phones, and lunch is eaten on the go. The only thing that's guaranteed to stop progress is the weather or high school sports.

Harvest is better than it used to be, though. My father's generation of farmers is marked by a huge number of missing fingers and even arms from accidents caused by corn pickers, the technology that preceded today's combines. Harvest didn't start until much later then, because we couldn't dry the corn mechanically and had to wait until it dried in the fields. A day when Dad picked 12 loads, or 1,200 bushels, was an exceedingly good one. Now we can pick 1,200 bushels an hour. Harvest was never done before Christmas in those times, and often lasted into the new year. This year, if the weather cooperates, we'll be done by Halloween.

But all frustrations aside, this job can be very satisfying. We dry our grain with large electric fans that push air up through the corn. They're powered by big electric motors that start with a sound very much like "Rhapsody in Blue," beginning at low growl and ending on a high note that lasts for months. The crescendo of a tin bin fan that marks the start of our harvest is an exciting sound to me. And in a year like this, with a good crop and beautiful weather, well, it just doesn't get any better.

Blake Hurst's family mostly grows corn and soybeans.

the
great
indoors

Model Fathers,
Trophy Sons

by Dave George

OAKFIELD, NEW YORK, JUNE 2004: The Pinewood Derby, in which Cub Scouts make and then race small wooden cars, is a rite of passage for many American boys—and a terror for plenty of fathers.

Pinewood Derby families fall into two categories. There are the ones who have trouble figuring out which side of the sandpaper you use. That's my group.

My father and I used a jackknife to shape our Derby car in 1970—not because we were handy with it, but because we didn't own any other tools—and then we spray-painted it. We were pretty proud . . . until Derby night. That's when we encountered the other class of kids—whose fathers were engineers, with basement wood shops more complete than some factories. They showed up carrying cars with multicolored paint jobs, weighed down with lead, wheels freshly lubed with silicone spray.

The first group went into shock at the sight of the second, so they've either suppressed all memories of the Pinewood Derby, or they remember in painful, exquisite detail how they lost to precision-engineered machines. This winter, I kept a Pinewood Derby diary—just so the doctors would know what happened if my son or I had a breakdown.

December 17: A dark pall descends over what had been a happy holiday season. . . . At his monthly pack meeting, my almost-seven-year-old son, Michael, received a Pinewood Derby kit. Earlier in the meeting, the pack made Christmas ornaments for needy families. Seeing the mess that Mikey and I made with mere construction paper and glue, I suggested that our ornament should go to a *blind* needy family. Now we're expected to make a raceable car?

January 17: Desperate after a month of denial, I do what every geeky modern father does when stumped: I go online. Finding a treasure trove of Pinewood advice on the Web, Mikey and I slide over to Hobby House Toys, where I buy some weights and a tube of graphite lubricant. This month, Mikey finally mastered zipping his coat—now he's going to combine these components into a winning machine?

February 8: It's time to cut the car. Because the Pinewood Derby is supposed to be a father-son project, I have Mikey in the basement with me. He goes to his Little Tikes plastic workbench and grabs some plastic tools, while I sketch a sleek aerodynamic design on the block of wood. Lacking a bench of my own, I tie some old sweatpants as padding around a metal pole in my basement. And since I don't have the scrap wood I'd have if I were a "real man," I use some paint-stirring sticks to protect the block of wood as I clamp the mess to the metal pole. Are those the tears of my shop teacher falling from heaven?

The wood keeps slipping under my borrowed coping saw (thank goodness for neighbors), resulting in a shape less Porsche-like than I'd imagined. I accidentally dig a big dent into the top of the car with the clamp, and leave behind several errant saw marks.

February 14: While Cupid shoots his arrows, I sit here with some 60-grit sandpaper, trying to get my—er, "our"—car in better shape.

February 28: The car is painted—blue and orange, just like Mike wanted—and looking good! I even use our oven to cure the paint.

March 2: I spray on two coats of clear sealant, and the car looks like glass. Then disaster strikes: I figure that if two coats look good, three will be better. Wrong. While curing coat three in the oven, the paint blisters in several places. My wife first cajoled me in from the window ledge, then talked me out of trying to fix the paint job.

March 5: We add the wheels! Wheel alignment is critical to Pinewood Derby success. Unfortunately, by the time the car crosses our kitchen floor, it's turned 90 degrees.

March 17: Derby Day. My first reaction was the same one I had 34 years ago: Our car is one of the ugliest and crudest there! Two brothers bring in vehicles that look exactly like a cell phone and a remote control, respectively. There are racers with paint jobs better than the one on my real car.

Then the cars are raced . . . and we win each heat! At the end of the night, Mikey squares off for the championship. He wins the first round and comes in second for the next two, finishing third overall!

That night we put Mikey to bed with his trophy on his dresser. When we looked in on him later, he'd moved it to a shelf right above his pillow.

Note to my own dad: We finally got our honor back.

When not building cars, Dave George recruits engineers in the Rochester, New York, area.

This Old House

by Blake Hurst

TARKIO, MISSOURI, DECEMBER 2002: We live in an agricultural region that has just endured a record drought. The stock market is in a swoon, as is the local economy. So my wife and I decided to celebrate by buying a house.

Mind you, our decision was made even tougher by family pressures.

Julie and I started married life in a four-room tenant house with no central heat or air-conditioning. The pipes froze with regularity, and the electric baseboard heaters were so expensive to run that we spent the first winter in two rooms, which we heated with a woodstove. The foundation of our home was made of soft brick that was crumbling in places, allowing easy entry to cold winds and rodents. One extremely large creature traveled up inside the wall and took up residence directly over our bed, scratching and keeping us awake each night. We attacked that rat with every trap, poison, and potion known to man, but he didn't leave his perch until the next spring. It was a testament to love that knows no bounds that my wife stuck with me for the three years we lived there.

When our second child was on the way, we purchased a house that was warmer, but sat above a basement that filled with water after every heavy dew. There was also the disapproval of my grandfather to deal with. He didn't think that any farmer should live in town, even a very small town like the one where this house was located. Grandpa finally came to visit only because it was the sole way he could see his great-grandkids.

Our third home came painted in a color scheme redolent of the 1970s drug culture. No surprise, as the previous resident ended up spending a hitch in the state penitentiary for some illegal farm diversification. This house was in the country, which pleased my grandfather, but it was built with used lumber, leaving our ceilings only seven and a half feet tall. Over the years we reroofed the house and added a couple of bedrooms, central air, a porch, new siding, and a redone kitchen.

But my wife and I have long nursed a dream, one that involves high ceilings, beautiful woodwork, formal gardens, and enough bookshelves to hold all the volumes I own. On a lark, we toured a house for sale in the town of Tarkio. The place turned out to have three stories, solid oak wainscoting, pocket doors, and beautiful wood floors. The two-acre lot looked like a bare palette for my wife's horticultural passions. And the house has a huge porch that's ideal for the kind of lavish hanging baskets only someone running a greenhouse business like ours can afford. After a thorough 15-minute discussion, we bought the house.

Julie and I are now violating an even deeper family taboo. You see, when I was about 14, my grandfather gave me a memorable object lesson. He took me by the home that my great-grandfather had built on a farm 30 miles from where we live now. That home stretched my ancestor financially to the point that trying to pay for it eventually caused him to lose his farm. My grandfather took that lesson so seriously that he lived in a rented house without running water until he was almost 60. He and my grandmother did finally build a home, but it was a very modest ranch structure that he no doubt paid for with cash.

In our family, capital has been used only for farmland and farm machinery for three generations. The home loan Julie and I took out will be the first mortgage in the family for nearly 100 years. The weight of the generations is on my shoulders, and it lies heavy.

We're excited about our new purchase, but the joy is tempered by the realization that my grandfather would not have been pleased. And not without some reason—after all, agriculture is, by its nature, a risky and capital-intensive business. Government estimates for the next decade place farming at the top of a dubious list: The occupation likely to experience the sharpest job losses. Grandpa had little formal education, but he was wise—in most things, including his frugality, he was absolutely right.

Julie and I realize that we're risking the progress of 25 years of extremely hard work. But we love old things, structures built to last, and style (the house is a Queen Anne, as near as we can tell). Our town is declining in population, and our new house needs owners who will care for her and help preserve a time when Tarkio was growing and gracious, and life moved at a slower speed. We'll take care of the house, grow gardens that are the envy of the neighbors, and finally have a place to entertain our rapidly growing extended family.

We'll work hard to rid ourselves of debt. In the meantime, I'm banking on the hope that Grandpa would be somewhat mollified by the fact that we're spending all this money to preserve a house that was built a hundred years ago. In the family tradition, that's got to count for something.

These days, Blake Hurst is spending lots of time in antique shops hunting for furniture.

Embracing Harriet

by Christine Parsons

"But what do at-home mothers actually do?"
— from the book *She Works/He Works: How Two-Income Families Are Happier, Healthier, and Better Off*

DANVILLE, CALIFORNIA, DECEMBER 2003: As I perused the library shelves, *She Works/He Works* dared me to slide it into my non-employed, stay-at-home-mom hands. I resisted. Pundits who have masseuses and headache-management specialists on staff might be able to handle the fiery arguments a book like that can open up . . . but I'm a full-time nurturer of adolescents, armed only with two Advils and a half-wrapped piece of sugarless gum buried in my purse.

This one-person debate was interrupted by my seventh-grader, Michelle, juggling Renaissance books for her research project. "Mom, I'm ready. Can we go?"

I nodded. And on impulse I grabbed the get-a-job-girl book. I told myself that I'd read it in short doses, take deep breaths, and not get sucked in. The librarian scanned Michelangelo, Bellini, and da Vinci, each swipe sending a high-pitched tone into the air. Finally came the feminist manifesto: *Beep!*

When we got home, Michelle set up shop at the kitchen table. I read from the counter a few steps away, in between chopping garlic and onions for the spaghetti.

The two full-time working-mom authors thanked the National Institute of Mental Health for the $1 million grant that had allowed them to study 300 full-time working couples (60 percent with children) over a four-year period. After three interviews with each member of this homogeneous group, the researchers concluded that stay-at-home-moms simply don't exist anymore.

The onions burned. *Wow,* I thought, *I'm extinct—dial telephones, albino squirrels, and me.*

My breathing quickened. I slapped pureed tomatoes and basil into the pot and scanned the first chapter: "Ozzie and Harriet Are Dead." The authors explained that as a single-income couple, Mr. and Mrs. Nelson represented "fear of change," an unhealthy "brand of family values," and a threat to "government policies that will help, not hinder, working families."

In real life, the Nelson clan did work, for 14 years, under studio lights and a tight production budget. And after all that, Rick Nelson found cocaine, left his wife and kids, and died in a plane crash. I plopped steaming pasta into six bowls, betting that Harriet wished for the scripted life where she stayed home, and Rick stayed swell right through puberty.

A few days later, family members had learned to flee whenever I entered a room with "The Book." I stomped about, cantankerous from study after study debunking the "Mom is best" myth, reassessing my life between loads of laundry. Maybe the make-a-buck, say-yes-to-day-care philosophy was good sense. Why fritter away years on the fruit of my womb when some minimum-wage chick could do it for me just fine?

"Why are you still reading that?" asked my husband, leaving me for his la-de-da doctor job. "You know it makes you feel lousy." Ignoring him, I squinted at the chapter facing me on the ledge over the sink. "Did you know that at-home-moms are depressed and die sooner than women with paying jobs?" I asked, icicles dripping from my words.

"I'd like to see the so-called study *that* tidbit came from," answered Mr. Scientific.

Sighing, I trudged down the hall to the dresser next to our bed. In the top drawer, under T-shirts and

sweatpants, I pulled out a letter my daughter had prop-
ped on my pillow a few years ago:

> *Dear Mom,*
>
> *I wanted to say why I love you. It's because
> you are always willing to help me if I get stuck.
> . . . You always make people feel at home if
> they're sleeping over or coming over to play. You
> don't make impolite comments about what I like
> or dislike. You understand a person's feelings . . .
> but most of all, you love me like I love you.*
>
> *Love,*
> *Michelle*

I returned the anti-mothering tome to the library
immediately. Free at last! And on my way out the
door, I spotted *Home by Choice: Raising Emotionally
Secure Children in an Insecure World* by Brenda Hunter,
Ph.D. It turns out I'm not endangered after all—41
percent of America's children under the age of 15 are
still cared for by their mothers at home.

And Dr. Hunter poses the important question
that *She Works/He Works* didn't dare ask: "What truly
matters in life? The love and affection that rolls across
the generations through our children, or how much
money we leave behind?"

Here's to mothering.

Christine Parsons writes for <u>The American Enterprise</u> only when she's not scrubbing oatmeal out of dishpans.

Casper Confessional

by Dale Anema

LITTLETON, COLORADO, DECEMBER 1998: Seven years ago I happened to sit down in a Casper, Wyoming, hotel bar at about 6:30 P.M. for complimentary hors d'oeuvres and a drink. A guy nearby loudly told a pretty good joke, which reminded the person next to me of the ones he knew. By 10:00, six of us were huddled at the end of the bar: a truck driver, an independent oilman, a financial analyst, a traveling salesman, the hotel's manager (our group's lone female), and me.

Jokes reminded us of life situations, and vice versa, and eventually we were truly baring our souls, describing successes and failures, hopes and disappointments, sins and nobility, delights and regrets. In one of those rare moments when personal facades drop, nothing was sacred—infidelities, lies, prejudices, ugly pride, fears, righteousness, and relationships with God were all matter-of-factly laid out on the bar. In fact, the jokes made the horror of some of the stories more chilling. Every word was carefully listened to; no praise or condemnation was forthcoming. And the stories were told with no apparent ego or humility.

The truck driver grew up in rural Georgia. When he was in high school, he and his friends cruised around looking for black men with white women or in white neighborhoods. They'd jump out of the car and beat the hapless young men within an inch of their lives. He said that they almost considered it a religious crusade. He now counted his dispatcher, a fellow driver, and two dockworkers who regularly load his truck—all blacks—among his best friends. He solemnly described the self-loathing he felt over these brutal, senseless acts of his youth.

The oilman quietly told us that when he was a wildcatter in his mid-20s, his neighbor informally invested in a three-well drilling pool. The first two were dusters, while the third came in marginally well. Our new friend had retained a quarter interest in the wells, and after paying the bills his share would barely cover his living expenses, not enough for him to keep his company afloat. So he told his neighbor that because of cost overruns, the first two wells had depleted the drilling fund, and he'd raised the money for the third well from additional investors. His neighbor never questioned the story—he just said it was a long shot anyway and thanked him for the opportunity.

Six months later the neighbor lost his job and was having a difficult time. The oilman wanted to help him out, but he wasn't yet doing that well himself. A couple of years passed, and his neighbor was killed in an auto accident. Our drinking buddy helped with the funeral expenses, and over the next several years occasionally gave money to the widow and her kids, but he never had the heart to tell them of his cheating. He blubbered as he related his haunted feelings—some nights, he told us, he didn't sleep at all.

The salesman said that his territory used to include Sacramento, California. He'd become quite friendly with a buyer there, and after seeing her professionally once a month for about a year, they began an affair. She became pregnant, and they split the cost of the abortion. Shortly thereafter, he was assigned a new territory so that he no longer had to deal with that untoward situation. His wife of five years had never found out. A few years later he was in the room when their first child was delivered. He felt some remorse for the abortion, but in his euphoria, he put it out of his mind.

As his daughter grew, the salesman's guilt began to overwhelm him. He spent almost every night in bars, even when he was in town. When he did see his wife and daughter, he was angry and distant. After several months of this, his wife suggested a trial separation . . . and he broke down and told her everything. She said that she'd suspected something like that, but she still loved him and wanted to stay married and provide a stable home for their daughter. He found another sales job that required less travel and spent every minute he could with his family—even though he felt unworthy of their love and devotion.

I recounted a situation I'd had 15 years before. I was having an affair with a divorced co-worker who had two children. She became pregnant twice (intentionally, I thought), and both times I said I wouldn't marry her. I didn't encourage or discourage abortions, but she had two. We later split up on nasty terms, and I had no contact with her or her kids from that day on.

Later, when I'd become a different person, I wanted to have a family with a lady I'd met—but the agony I'd caused began to torment me. Not only was I responsible for snuffing out the lives of my own babies, but also for adding incredible misery to two other children. I prayed for forgiveness daily, but still had a gnawing feeling that it was too little, too late. The pernicious choices I'd made fostered irreparable harm that I feared would haunt me the rest of my life, and perhaps thereafter.

We confessors were interrupted by the clatter of dishes and murmur of the breakfast crowd. It was suggested we eat together, but I think we all knew that the magical hours were over. It was one of those evenings that can never be duplicated.

I wonder what became of those people. I never saw any of them again, but they're always on my mind—because that night, they were all so openly human that I could see their hearts beating.

Dale Anema negotiates land leases across the western U.S. for mineral companies.

School
in the Dining Room

by Isabel Lyman

Pelham, Massachusetts, September 2001: On a wintry morning, two masculine heads are hovering over a textbook on my scuffed dining-room table. The heads begin talking about radicals. No, not the Che Guevara or Abbie Hoffman kind—rather, those familiar to students of algebra. Willard III, who is 15 and goes by the family nickname "Bebé," is being taught by his father and namesake, Willard II (who goes by the nickname "Wid"). My husband's tools for teaching his son math are old-fashioned but effective—pencil, paper, and oodles of sample problems. He requires mastery before advancement.

For the past year, Wid has worked part-time as a house painter and laborer while training for triathlons, but he devotes the bulk of his day to homeschooling Bebé. In addition to algebra, he conducts classes in physical science, the Bible, and Dirt Biking 101. On occasion, he'll invite Mr. Bach, Mr. Chopin, and Mr. Rachmaninoff to provide background concertos for his classes. He also escorts our younger child around western Massachusetts and southern Vermont to ice-hockey games and snowboarding excursions.

I pitch in by dispensing fiction and nonfiction reading assignments, as well as checking compositions and driving Bebé to his job at a service station. The three of us often watch news shows such as *The O'Reilly Factor* together and discuss current events. One day a week, Bebé attends an American-history seminar at the Victorian home of Whitney Robinson, age 14, a fellow homeschooler who lives nearby. Whitney is taught by her lawyer dad, who delivers the succinct weekly lectures.

Our family has been homeschooling for more than a decade, and no year has resembled the previous one. Dan, our elder son, was taught at home for many semesters while we lived on a small farm with chickens and cows. During a subsequent year, we went on sabbatical to Oklahoma and received a crash course in tornadoes and Sooners. When Dan turned 16, he yearned to try public school and play football, so we grudgingly agreed to this experiment in school choice. His experience—he just graduated from Amherst Regional High School—has only confirmed our opinion of government schools as tax-funded temples to socialism and adolescent foolishness.

My husband has worked as a high school teacher, a college math instructor, and a long-haul trucker. I think of him as a contemporary Renaissance man, one of the few Americans who holds both a Ph.D. in civil engineering and a CDL (Commercial Driver's License) for driving 18-wheelers. Last summer, when I accepted a job in the editorial department of a big-city newspaper, Wid seized the moment to enthusiastically reinvent himself as Mr. Schoolmarm. Not only did he teach Bebé, but he also volunteered at a homeschool cooperative (the only male amidst a sea of moms), teaching other teens Español and math. In addition, he sorted laundry, threw football passes to Dan, mowed the lawn, and frequently brought me bagels and iced coffee for lunch.

After my newspaper stint, I turned my attention to writing a book. When the votes came in, there was an overwhelming consensus that Wid should continue being "all Dad, all the time." So the Lymans supplemented their living expenses by drawing down earlier investments in real estate and the stock market.

Our lifestyle sometimes raises eyebrows and provokes pointed questions. Even in an age where clergy, cops, and social thinkers often lament the dearth of good fathers, alpha males turned homeschooling dads are a strange species. So, when Dr. Lyman explains to folks why he doesn't have "a real job," he simply says, "My family is my job . . . at least for now." He's investing his time, energy, and talents in his younger son's academic education and his older son's character training. He wears the hats of teacher, principal, custodian, bus driver, coach, guidance counselor, and editor.

Wid remains unfazed by the questions he's asked, and I'm honored to have our family on the receiving end of all this stability. There certainly are tangible results to his efforts: Dan had impressive SAT scores and got accepted into the college of his choice; two of Bebé's tough hockey teammates have asked their parents to homeschool them; and our boys often spot grammar gaffes and debunk politically correct platitudes. And they've learned to value blue-collar, white-collar, and open-collar workers.

As for the future, Dan is pondering a job in advertising and marketing. Bebé, who has money tucked away in trucking stocks, wants to create lots of wealth before he gets married. He says he wants to be available to homeschool his children. Hmm . . . I wonder where he got such a radical idea?

Isabel Lyman is the author of <u>The Homeschooling Revolution</u>.

Multiculturalism
Brooklyn-Style

by Joseph Jacobs

BROOKLYN, NEW YORK, OCTOBER 1996: For 80 years I lived the "multicultural" experience. My parents were uneducated immigrants from Lebanon who came here as adolescents nearly 100 years ago. Their familiar language and that of our ethnic enclave in Brooklyn was Arabic. But all seven of us children went to public schools where we spoke English, even to children from other Lebanese families.

Our family had none of today's multicultural conflicts. When Mom and Dad spoke to us, often in Arabic, we answered in English. Lebanon was a wonderful country of nostalgic memory, but the United States was our home, our future, and especially our opportunity.

My parents had no problem harmonizing warm memories of their beautiful homeland with gratitude for the freedom and opportunity in their cherished adopted country. We children admired the freedom that attracted our parents away from the cruel Ottoman rulers of their homeland. We knew we must be well educated so that we could join the mainstream of American culture; A's in English were expected.

When I visited Lebanon, I saw the destructive potential of multiculturalism. I'd seen hints of it among the Lebanese in Brooklyn, but the overwhelming sense of being American made tribal rivalries trivial. My parents' country, I quickly realized, was actually destroyed by multiculturalism.

Divided by 13 different tribal loyalties, the Lebanese are a caricature of what extreme multiculturalism can do. Fifteen years of suicidal intertribal fighting laid the people prostrate, only to be "rescued" by Syrian intervention. Although the Lebanese are some of the most sophisticated and best-educated people in the Middle East, they have difficulty acknowledging that they owe primary allegiance to their country rather than to their tribes.

In America, by contrast, our great strength as a nation has been the unification of successive waves of "hungry" immigrants. Despite the natural tendency to huddle together in ethnic enclaves, the lure of the melting pot made us all Americans first. We were taught to cherish our ancient heritages at home and in our local communities. But we were also taught to cherish America in school and in the broader community.

Today, multiculturalism has infected academia, and grade schools practice bilingual education. Based on my experience in Brooklyn, it's unquestionably wrong.

Bilingual education is a shining example of compassion gone wrong. Is it painful for a child raised in a home where only Spanish is spoken to learn English? Of course it is, but no more so than learning to spell or to do arithmetic. Is it kind to spare him the pain of learning English? Hardly. Turning him out into an English-speaking society believing that English is a second language—*that* is cruel.

Now the extension of this faulty thinking includes the printing of multilingual voter ballots, bringing disunity to one of democracy's central rituals. Need we apologize for asking those who come here to adapt to our common culture? After all, opportunities for immigrants' children were and are unbounded, as my family and so many others have demonstrated.

Of course, if you don't like the American experience, you can always move to the Middle East and enjoy all the multiculturalism you want.

Joseph Jacobs is the author of <u>The Compassionate Conservative</u> and <u>The Anatomy of an Entrepreneur</u>.

Tall Latte,
Hold the Rudeness

by Susanna Luddy

WASHINGTON, D.C., MARCH 2001: In the early mornings I enjoy walking my baby girl through the neighborhood, getting coffee, and watching her absorb the world around us. During a recent Starbucks stop, the woman in front of me felt that she'd been waiting too long and barked at the young man behind the counter. He apologized profusely, yet she continued to scold him to the point of embarrassment.

I stood there holding my one-year-old daughter, Jocelyn, wondering if she was noticing this woman's behavior. Then I thought about the previous day at MotoPhoto, where Jocelyn had witnessed another woman screaming at an employee, and last week at a gift shop, where she'd watched the store manager berate a customer. I wondered how long it would be before my little girl decides that rudeness is acceptable.

Right then at Starbucks, I decided to take a stand. I said to the impolite woman, "They're busy and working very hard, and I think you were rude."

She turned to me and my daughter and snarled, "Well, you may be able to sit around all day with your baby, but I have to get to work." Then she stormed off. As I left the store still in disbelief, she drove up to me and shouted, "Mind your own business!"

Clearly this woman thought that my business was to go home and sit around all day. Au contraire— beyond my new crusade of promoting civility in this busy city, I'm a mother. I'm responsible for shaping the character of a child, forming a young person who (I hope) will never imitate the rudeness she's hearing all around her.

Since she was born, it seems as if every time I've been dressed nicely and rushing out the door with her, Jocelyn has spit up or needed a diaper change. But I clean her up as fast as I can, hug her, and tell her that I love her. My schedule is much less important than her feelings. I want her to learn that when we're frustrated or rushing, it's not a license to be unkind to others.

I often hear people snap at a clerk, "Give me a tall coffee!" Is it so much trouble to instead ask kindly, "May I please have a tall coffee?" When I hand my daughter her bottle, I tell her to say "Thank you" in the hopes that she'll learn to repeat the phrase and understand its importance. Currently, she grabs it and sticks it in her mouth like she hasn't had a drink for a week, but we're working on it.

When I first gave her cookies, I'd break them in two and ask, "A piece for Mommy, please?" Now she won't eat anything without offering me some as well—she's learned to enjoy sharing.

Sometimes, however, Jocelyn tests me. I've spied on her in her crib: She'll stand there and scream for a minute, then sit down quietly and wait for me to come running. When she doesn't hear me, she stands up and screams again. It would be easier to give in to her than to listen to her scream. But if she doesn't learn who's in charge now, when will she develop an understanding of authority or respect for others?

There are impolite and disorderly people in the world, and I don't want my child to become one. I want her to be accountable for her actions. But empathy doesn't arise spontaneously in children. It's nurtured and developed with patience and creativity—and not by parents who sit around all day.

Susanna Luddy, a Realtor and freelance writer, raises Jocelyn in Washington, D.C.

Only in a Small Town

by Hendrik Mills

HARLEM, MONTANA, DECEMBER 1997: I'm a mechanic at a tire- and auto-repair garage in rural Montana, and it's as if I work in a Norman Rockwell painting. We don't have a potbellied stove to heat us through our long winters, but aside from that detail, it's more or less a *Saturday Evening Post* cover come to life whenever, say, Bill Stuart comes in the door.

Bill is almost 70, and he rarely has anything fixed by us. He doesn't have to, as he has his own well-outfitted workshop at home. Like a lot of men around here, he mastered the arts of welding, tinkering, big-rig driving, and other useful rural skills long ago. An ex-farmer and school-bus driver, Bill makes a daily (or even twice-daily) visit to our garage, lasting anywhere from ten minutes to an hour. He helps himself to our coffee, then, paying no attention to the "liability and insurance issues" that keep customers out of the back rooms of big-city repair garages, walks into the work area to see what we're up to.

Bill may offer updates on the high-water situation around Thirty-Mile Creek, which has been flooding near where he lives; his comments are added to the reports and speculations on local creeks and dams already being tossed about by patrons standing around watching their pickups or tractor tires get worked on. Like many customers, Bill feels free to rest his elbows on the fender of whatever vehicle I'm currently toiling over, and to stick his head under the hood. He offers advice about the car, perhaps even information about its owner. Then he'll ask me something like, "Is that big black thing over there the computer?" Or something about the vehicle will recall a story, perhaps about the days when he had a whole crew of men driving grain trucks for him. He doesn't repeat his stories.

If there's one thing an auto mechanic likes, other than being paid, it's being admired for competence in fixing broken cars when others can't. A mechanic likes to preserve some mystery about "how I do it" to guard his arcane knowledge and back-room procedures. This way, all the customer sees is the miraculous appearance (after several hours of who knows what) of his repaired car, now humming reassuringly.

In our shop we charge $30 an hour, and in many cases the customers just have to trust that we're really working steadily and skillfully to fix the short in their wiring or the glitch in their fuel-injection system. If there's a $120 labor charge on a work order, we all want to feel that each second was spent productively on the problem. That's why, when I first came to this rural outpost to live and ply my trade, I didn't much like having the customer, his wife and two children, Bill Stuart, Skrud Brekke, and the rancher waiting to have his truck tire repaired all watching me scratch my head over the customer's wiring problem—and even offering pointers on how to resolve it!

It tended to irritate and annoy me considerably when, as I studied the wiring diagram for the car in question and poked my voltmeter leads here and there, Bill would casually point to a connector and ask, "Why don't you try plugging that red wire back together?" and then pull deeply on his cigarette while watching my response.

Sometimes I get to explain to the ignorant bystanders that the whosiwhatsit has nothing to do with the whatchamacallit. But other times the dratted bystanders are right! This sort of thing tends to erode one's treasured image as an expert who knows things that the layman couldn't possibly understand. Most city mechanics would find this sort of daily interference maddening, perhaps even intolerable, as I once did.

But can city mechanics leave their own cars parked outside all day unlocked with the keys in them? If a customer can't get there before closing time, can urban tradesmen leave a minivan on the lot and be able to count on the customer to come in later and pay the bill? When it's bitterly cold, can you go to the local grocery store and see a row of cars idling at the curb while their owners shop inside, not a bit worried about their unlocked cars? In anonymous cities, if your vehicle is stuck in the snow, can you hail the first passerby by name and get pulled out? If you want a word with your state representative, do you just wait a few weeks until he comes in with a flat in the back of his pickup, boots smeared with cow manure, and hang around for a chat? All of these things happen, and are thought normal, in our small ranching community.

I first came to accept observation and intervention on the part of village bystanders as a necessary evil, the price I was willing to pay to live here. But then I began to notice that even when they've seen us stumped and confused, our shop's customers and drop-in visitors don't judge the mechanics harshly as long as we persist and eventually fix the car. Customers don't watch us maliciously with lawsuits on their mind. And they'd just rather stand and watch the mechanics struggle with their pickups, amidst the loud racket and questionable chemicals, than sit around reading old magazines in the waiting room. You can look at it as community participation, not interference.

These kibitzers can even be useful. For example, a few days ago Bill helped me force the air out of a customer's brakes by sitting in the cab and pumping the brake pedal while I opened the bleeder screws. Later that afternoon he showed up with his power bleeder, a device that permits one man alone to do the job. He's going to let me use it, he said, because his leg had gotten sore from all that pedal stomping in the morning.

My wife and I hope to buy the garage I work in from Paul, the 78-year-old founder and owner. We won't make many changes. And we won't put up a sign that says NO CUSTOMERS ALLOWED IN WORK AREA.

Hendrik Mills enjoys small-town life with his wife and children.

Inner Drives
on the Hard Drive

by Marilyn Penn

NEW YORK, NEW YORK, MAY 2003: I started playing Scrabble over the Internet last year. It's allowed me to make some interesting discoveries—about games, about the people who play them, and about the influence of the World Wide Web.

Players on the **games.com** site I use must register their "handles" if they want to be rated. This offers a double bonus: a chance for self-expression, plus complete anonymity. Names range from the benign to the salacious, with many permutations in between.

I've played with "cheater" (he was), "sexylegs" (a strong player despite the image), and "mywayisall" (a quitter when it wasn't). I've learned to be wary of players who've given themselves aggressive names (like "warlord")—not because their owners play more fiercely, but because they seem to get vindictive when they fall behind.

You'd think that people who enjoy a cerebral, sedentary pastime such as Scrabble would be on the gentle side of the human spectrum—after all, lovers of vocabulary aren't your stereotypical swimmers with sharks. But we get our share of bad losers: If an online Scrabble player decides not to move at all, for instance, there's nothing his opponent can do to force him. If the board is idle long enough, both players will be disconnected, and both will have points deducted from their rating. This fault allows a spiteful loser to prevent the victor from profiting from his conquest.

Players are also highly competitive, which is a good thing for those who wish to keep honing their skills. Many of the most unusual words I've picked up have been at the losing end, as my opponent whipped out *gloze, killdee, woald,* or *jiao.*

But I wasn't prepared for the nastiness on the chat bar, the malicious sabotaging of games, or the lewdness of what I hope are adolescents blowing off steam. These ugly aspects of my hobby are entirely by-products of playing on the Web, I've decided. The Internet is like a masked ball—you can act out your wildest fantasies without being recognized or stigmatized. This fuels unstable people to misbehave more freely, more often.

Anonymity bestows power on insecure people. And the Internet facilitates immediate exposure and gratification for show-offs. Last week, some pervert sullied the air with a riff about defecation and sex that lasted for about 20 minutes—there was no one to shut him up, and no way to boot him off. Other players will occasionally object to the prurience, but that often just gives the closet exhibitionist an extra thrill. I'm surprised that people choose a Scrabble site for these displays, but perhaps they get an additional frisson from shocking quiet people.

Playing any game online allows an individual the privacy to cheat. You can always tell when someone is looking up a word before deciding whether to challenge—there's a time lag before the challenge button is pushed. Some cheaters use a word descrambler on another Website, something you obviously couldn't do in person. If you aren't competitive about your own ratings, playing against a partner aided by a computer can make the game more challenging . . . of course, the game then becomes completely one-sided and unfair. Quitting when you're losing is another low tactic. Quitters prevent the other guy from gaining points, even if he's earned them. This is generally not tolerated in face-to-face games.

On the Web, though, no one knows who you are, and you're free to abrogate the rules of good sportsmanship and revert to a more primal state. Recently I played against a woman who was 200 points behind. She refused to go gently into that good night, and instead kept putting her letters in places that connected high-scoring words, effectively creating nonsense. The first time she did this I challenged her, and of course her word was removed. By the third time I decided to let her get away with *quiverwvjoust* (80 points), because I realized that she'd keep on doing it, and I really just wanted to end the game.

On the positive side, having played with participants from all over the world, I can say that most people are friendly, spirited, and conscientious. I've locked horns with students, grandpas, young mothers, and people at work (I hope they're on their lunch hour). One day I had some carpet cleaners in my home, and while I waited for them to finish, I logged on to a game. One of the workers, a strapping young bodybuilder, kept glancing over at what I was doing. Assuming that he hadn't seen this site before, I proceeded to explain.

"I know," he replied, "I play it, too. I was just looking at your moves to see if I agreed with what you were doing."

My favorite opponent was a Korean man playing from Seoul. His chats were formal and revealed that he hadn't been raised speaking English. Nevertheless, he was beating me handily, and close to the end of the game, when there were just a few tiles left, I conceded that he'd win since I was holding the "q" with no place to put it. "I shall try to make a space for you," he said with grace, and he did.

I played my "q," but was delighted that he won anyway. He didn't abandon decency just because no one knew who he was. He carried it the extra mile, to a grand gesture of gallantry. I shall remember that much longer than the score of any win I'll ever attain.

Marilyn Penn recently scored 284 points for one word in online Scrabble.

Fire

by Blake Hurst

ARKIO, MISSOURI, JUNE 1997: The floor joists in the house where I grew up were native walnut. In 1970, we tore down that house, and I spent the summer pulling out nails with a crowbar and stacking lumber. My father used those beautiful walnut boards, along with the wood we'd salvaged from two other houses on our farm, to build a new home in 1971.

The foundations of the three old houses were made from a soft red brick that had been fired more than a hundred years earlier in a local kiln. Those bricks kept my brother and me busy for another summer, as we knocked off the mortar and hauled them up to the site of the new home, where they were used for a fireplace. Dad hired a mason to build a foundation and lay those bricks that I hated so much, but he did the rest of the work himself.

While the house was under construction, we spent a summer and fall living in a place with no running water and no heat except for a woodstove. The five of us lived in four rooms with a privy out back. I spent a couple of months that fall in an ankle-to-hip cast, and the trips down the hill to the outhouse on icy terrain with crutches were enough to cure me forever of any romantic notions about the "good old days."

Anyway, last month my parents' home burned to the ground.

The fire started in late afternoon, while the family was home. Mom, Dad, and my grandfather were able to get out without injury. The house almost immediately filled with smoke, and no one could enter it, including the firefighters with their protective gear. We cut a hole in the wall of my father's office with a chainsaw and saved some of his business records, but were unable to go any further.

Fires are fought here in northwest Missouri by volunteer fire departments. We had firemen from two neighboring towns, an ambulance from a third, and a squad from a fourth town's power company. The firemen arrived quickly and worked very hard, at personal risk, but were unable to slow the blaze at all. There were dozens of spectators, all of whom had different ideas about firefighting, and advice flowed freely. But the blaze started in the basement and spread rapidly, and all efforts to put it out failed miserably. It was clear within an hour that my folks would lose everything.

Almost everyone who offered condolences to my father and mother spoke about the pictures they lost, or Mom's wedding ring, or all of the keepsakes that accrue like barnacles over 40 years of marriage. But what *I* miss most are those stupid bricks, the fireplace mantel that Dad fashioned from those walnut timbers, and the room divider made from the staircase spindles of my father's boyhood home.

We built the house as a family, and it was a testament to our ability to work together, as well as to my father's talent as a craftsman. When I drive today through the suburbs of Omaha and Kansas City, I see homes that are grander than that simple farmhouse, but their construction is shoddy in comparison. Those houses will change hands every few years, as corporations move employees, residents divorce, and people retire to planned communities. My folks' place, on the other hand, was built for their lifetime, and they fully expected that one of their grandchildren would live in it after they were gone.

Within 48 hours of the fire, my parents had heard from hundreds of relatives, neighbors, and friends. The Baptist church cooked enough food to feed the multitudes, and the Lutherans outfitted my parents in new clothes. I don't know if you can draw any theological conclusions from the differing reactions of the two congregations, but both followed the biblical injunction to care for the homeless.

Mom and Dad stayed with my wife and me until they found a house to rent, and we spent the first weekend after the fire brewing coffee for family, friends, and one Mary Kay cosmetics saleslady who, realizing that my mother was in the market for, well, everything, didn't want to let a sales opportunity pass her by. My mother handled the unrequested makeover with aplomb.

My father can fix anything that breaks on our farm, and when my brothers and I began farming ourselves, he often spent days doing nothing except repairing what we'd destroyed through the carelessness that seems to plague maledom until well into middle age. My mother was just as competent at mending the emotional bumps and bruises of young men facing the world with a surfeit of testosterone and a deficit of good sense. We've always relied on the intelligence, wisdom, and wit of my parents, so knowing what to say when my mother complains of being homesick is not easy.

My parents' home wasn't just the headquarters of our extended family, but it was also the heart of our family farm. Nothing has been accomplished on Hurst Farms in the past 25 years without first being argued about in Mom's kitchen. Without a fixed place to plan the day's work and solve the problems of the world (along with the local football and basketball teams), we're at a loss. Consequently, my parents will have no choice but to rebuild on the same spot. And soon.

That is, of course, assuming they can eventually agree on a house plan.

Blake Hurst never met an old house he didn't like.

Specially Ill Educated

by Kelly Rossiter

POULSBO, WASHINGTON, APRIL 1996: I'm a teacher at a junior high school, but I don't educate. Instead, I watch helplessly as a small group of students wreak havoc. This damage is the result of federal laws that seek to incorporate disabled students into the regular curriculum and expand the traditional definition of *disabled*. In combination, these laws create a reaction more explosive than anything ever seen in chemistry class.

Students with any loosely defined set of "behavioral difficulties" now receive civil-rights protection, and they can't be disciplined for these "difficulties."

Fearing the wrath of parental-advocacy groups and their lawyers, schools nationwide have therefore been brought to an educational standstill. Federal law specifically states that handicapped students must be placed in the "least restrictive environment," so that "to the maximum extent appropriate, children with disabilities are educated with children who are not disabled."

When I say "handicapped," what image comes to mind? Blind, autistic, epileptic? Well, I've walked miles shadowing my charges while they destroy school property, bang on classroom windows, and scream obscenities to both students and staff. These students are not mobility-limited, blind, or mute. No, they're what federal law calls "behaviorally disabled," a loose category of students who receive the educational equivalent of diplomatic immunity.

So what constitutes a "behavioral disability"? To quote my district's psychological evaluation form: "Section 504 does not set forth a list of specific diseases and conditions . . . because of the difficulty in ensuring the comprehensiveness of such a list." Among the general guidelines offered instead include: "An inability to learn which cannot be explained by intellectual, sensory, or health factors. . . . Inappropriate types of behavior or feelings under normal circumstances."

Certainly some student misbehavior can be traced to an actual physiological affliction, but most "inappropriate behavior" I see is exhibited by students who have control over their actions.

The federal legislation that started this problem has been around since the mid-1970s, so why the sudden turmoil? Well, your tax dollars and the legal system are hard at work here. Parent-advocacy groups backed by phalanxes of attorneys and funding from the Department of Education are prodding parents to sue. And many whose children misbehave are more than happy to blame the schools.

So you get scenarios like the one in California's Ocean View School District: Jimmy P., a student with a communicative disorder, had a history of attacking students, kicking staff members, and biting teachers. Claiming that the school set him up for failure, Jimmy's father refused to allow him to be removed from mainstream classrooms. The school sought an injunction to override his objection—although the injunction passed in state court, a federal court overruled it, saying that the injuries caused by Jimmy weren't serious enough to warrant removal.

I've seen teenagers who failed all their classes because they refused to open a book, who smashed a picture frame because they were "pissed off," who told the school principal to "go f--k your slutty mother." Even with an army of aides it's impossible to prevent this behavior, when "behaviorally disabled" students know that no disciplinary measures can be taken.

But it's happening now with your tax dollars, in your schools, in the name of civil rights.

According to many of my students, I'm a dumb s---head. But I'm smart enough to recognize that today's special-ed practices are a tragedy. The exorbitant price tag on current special education takes funds away from other students. Mainstream classes in some schools are dragged down by classroom chaos. And "behaviorally disabled" students are excused from any responsibility for their actions on civil-rights grounds.

Recently, while trying to talk one of my students I'll call "Mark" down from his desktop perch, where he stood simulating masturbation in front of the class, I heard this explanation: "Don't lecture me, Mr. Rossiter. I'm behaviorally disabled—I can't listen to lectures because they make me angry. And I can't control my anger."

Neither can I, Mark. Neither can I.

Kelly Rossiter lives and teaches near Seattle, Washington.

Burger Queen
by Erin Sharp

ITHACA, NEW YORK, JUNE 1999: When I announced the change of my major at Cornell from biology with pre-med aspirations to English, my advisor simply raised an eyebrow and asked if I planned to work at McDonald's for the rest of my life.

"Actually," I quipped, "I've been working at McDonald's for two and a half years, and it's sort of fun." His surprise was evident, a typical reaction to my shocking side occupation. I spoke the truth, though: I've held a dozen jobs ranging from camp counselor to pathologist's assistant (now including,

I suppose, freelance journalism), yet none have been as entertaining as my stints at the Golden Arches.

My double life as Miss Erin Sharp, Ivy League McDonald's Worker, has revealed twin stereotypes to me. People told that I go to Cornell view me as bright and ambitious; but put me behind the counter at McDonald's, and I'm usually assumed to be a high school dropout with 15 unseen piercings.

When I was six years old, McDonald's was my favorite place to eat, and kids haven't changed much in the last dozen years. I'm often asked by kids whether I've actually met "The Ronald" McDonald, and I've been given letters to pass along to him, like one of Santa's elves. Among kids, McDonald's workers rank right up there with police officers and firefighters.

Yet this perspective rarely survives adolescence. Respect for the workers of the fast-food industry is lost among most adults, with absurd results. Many so-called grown-ups seem to assume that McWorkers are stupid, so they attempt to scam us out of free food and coupons. The depths of tackiness to which some human beings will stoop in order to save a few pennies at a drive-through window are worthy of *Candid Camera*.

Grown men driving Lincoln Town Cars have bickered with me for five minutes over a measly ten-cent increase in the price of an Egg McMuffin. Perhaps they imagine that I overcharge each patron and hoard misbegotten dimes in a piggy bank behind the shake machine? My store once even received a phone call at noon from a furious woman demanding reimbursement for the breakfast she'd bought that morning; apparently, it was cold when she arrived at work . . . more than an hour later.

Yet our most famous TIC (Truculent, Irate Customer) lost her temper when we couldn't (in her eyes, *wouldn't*) provide the grilled-chicken sandwich she craved in the middle of breakfast rush hour. An entirely new traffic pattern was created next to the drive-through for the 25 minutes spent in fruitless argument and accommodation attempts by our managers while the grill team thawed frozen meat, heated a grill to cook on, and finally produced the coveted sandwich for her. When at last presented with it, she lofted the bag triumphantly and accused us of withholding it from her for the entire time, then zoomed off with these words: "I'm never coming back here again!" The effectiveness of this condemnation was tempered by her license plate, which proclaimed her to be from Delaware—more than an hour away.

A small portion of our patrons are so confused that there's really nothing to do but wait for them to leave. The most prominent example of this sort of "guest" is the infamous Snack Attack Lady, who ordered hotcakes and sausage during our 90-second-guaranteed-service hour and then ate her breakfast right outside the drive-through window. Heedless of the frenzied honking behind her, she carefully opened the platter, poured a puddle of syrup, rolled the sausage in a hotcake, and dipped both daintily into the syrup. My co-workers and I watched in speechless amazement. When asked what she was doing, she rolled her eyes and snapped, "What does it look like I'm doing? I'm eating my breakfast!" That woman has permanently forfeited all rights to complain about slow drive-through service.

And yet, there are some great customers out there, like the "Morning Crew": the seven retired men and one active police officer who wait for our doors to open every day so that they can enjoy their dawn coffee and conversation. If I miss a day of work, I return to inquiries about my health and concern that all was well. The greatest customers ever to grace our store were two deliverymen who drove up to the window one spring afternoon two years ago with armfuls of roses for my co-worker and me. They were moving their business out of state, they explained, and wanted to thank us for making their afternoons brighter.

Well, boys, if you're reading this article, thank you again for that fabulous surprise. I still have the ribbon that bound them.

Erin Sharp attended Cornell University.

Life with Father

by Karina Rollins

WASHINGTON, D.C., SEPTEMBER 2004: My father never tossed a softball with me. He never took me hiking. He never taught me how to start a campfire.

Thank goodness.

Had he been the type of person to do those things, he wouldn't have been the exceptional force in my life that he is. My father was the 14-year-old kid who spent his allowance on a record player and classical LPs, making him an outcast and bona fide nerd. Later, despite looks that put Cary Grant to shame, he was still a loner, swimming against the tide, devouring records and books along the way.

Since I was little, we listened to music together, and continue to do so to this day. My father opened the glorious world of classical music to me, but that's not the only type we listened to. It wasn't at a party at a friend's house, but on the sofa in our living room, sitting next to my father, that I first heard Pink Floyd, Bruce Springsteen, and The Alan Parsons Project.

Our huge living room was essentially a library with a couch, television set, and (superb) hi-fi, including a subwoofer that my father built himself. The walls were lined with the bookshelves and record cabinets that my father designed. My friends were in awe of the sheer volume of books and records that filled the room, and I basked in a feeling of superiority when I thought of their barren homes with not much more reading material than a *TV Guide* and the perfunctory Bible.

At our house, my atheist father stocked the library with multiple Bibles, since one of his many intellectual pursuits was biblical scholarship. Always one to share the delights of his mind with his daughter, he read me bedtime stories from the Old Testament.

When I was in the fifth grade, I wanted to go to Sunday school, and my father drove me every week. He once told me, as a thought experiment, to consider that there are two things God can't do: He can't make a square that's round, and He can't make an object so heavy that He can't lift it. I blabbed that witticism to my Sunday-school teacher, sweet-hearted Mr. Hall, who worried for my soul and told me I was obviously repeating those words from someone who wanted to keep me from God.

If he only knew—I thought my father *was* God.

As an adult, both of my parents continue to watch over my welfare. When my mother visits, she brings my favorite wine, cleans my apartment, and inspects the fridge to make sure I'm eating right. My dad brings books and magazines bulging with Post-it notes marking the pages he wants me to read. He wouldn't notice if I didn't eat for a week, but he makes sure that I have excellent stereo equipment and don't run low on CDs.

One might call my father decent to a fault. A chain-smoker, if he finishes a cigarette and there's no trash can nearby, he puts it out on the sole of his shoe and puts the butt in his pocket, leaving all his pockets full of burn holes and loose tobacco. When he goes shopping and fishes for change to pay the cashier, he ends up strewing bits of tobacco on the counter with the coins. Am I embarrassed when this happens? Bite your tongue! I'd be embarrassed if he threw his butts on the sidewalk like everyone else.

My father is an imperfect man: He stores news-papers in his kitchen cabinets, doesn't clean his house, and hauls home bags of books and magazines from his regular Barnes & Noble excursions, adding to the ever-increasing piles of brain food in every room in the house. He can be difficult and irritable and admittedly selfish.

My father is also the man who made up a special lullaby for me, which he sang to me every night, year after year, until I turned ten and felt too old for such things. My father is the man who always pushed me (and still does) to think critically, to strive for knowledge, and to settle for no less than the truth. It's because of my father that I love Stravinsky and Civil War history and *Star Wars*. I can't catch a softball, but I know how to shop for audio equipment and solder speaker wire together.

A daughter's life doesn't get better than that.

Karina Rollins is a senior editor of <u>The American Enterprise</u>, but she'll always remain her daddy's little girl.

Nursery Lessons

by Brian Connelly

PITTSBURGH, PENNSYLVANIA, MARCH 2003: I'm a man who worked in high-quality professional child care for four years. I can't really recommend it to anyone—especially children.

I'd been working at a freelance job when my wife got pregnant, and teaching children seemed like a great alternative to chasing more irregular, part-time jobs. We also thought that the staff discount at an expensive child-care center in Pittsburgh's East End could be a great way to pay for our own child's care—a thought we soon reconsidered.

On my first day I was told that the children would address me by my first name in order to avoid the feeling of a hierarchy. They in turn should never be called "Honey," "Buddy," or silly nicknames. Children couldn't be put in a time-out, or disciplined in any way that seemed like punishment. And one should never say, "Be quiet down there, you two," as this was considered too scary. Instead, we'd go with, "Some friends are having trouble listening."

The guidelines made it clear: Children at this high-priced center were under no obligation to listen to an adult—they were the autonomous customers of a neutral provider. Those are very different rules from the ones most of us knew in childhood; inevitably, the result is going to produce very different grown-ups.

When they'd meet me at the child-care center, mothers (never fathers) often said, "You have such an important job." Considering that they were all dropping their kids off on the way to some other job that they seemed to consider *more* important, it became a bad joke. The "critical" nature of day-care work, I realized, was on the order of a garbageman. Yup, it's very important that the trash be picked up. Imagine if it wasn't—you might actually have to deal with it yourself. Who wants that?

Some of the moms who were pleased to see me thought that their youngsters would listen better to a male voice. They *did* want their kids to listen . . . they just didn't want them to be disciplined.

in real life

222

Day care is bad enough as an economic necessity; as an ideology, it's insufferable. The pseudo-scientific concepts and language that buttress this service industry for children have now permeated American families. Parents now talk about themselves and other adults as "caregivers," as if children have a medical condition requiring specialized knowledge. The word reduces adult relationships with children to mere safekeeping. Other roles—like moral guide, discipliner, teacher—consequently fade.

Thanks to media portrayals and peer pressure, the therapeutic child-care model is changing what it means to be an adult and to be a child. Language is hesitant and unsure nowadays. Parents no longer say, "Pick up your toys"; instead, they ask, "Wouldn't it be better if we cleaned up now?" A mother got angry with me because I told her five-year-old to take her doughnut to the table. "You used the imperative," the woman said, glaring.

The problem is that children don't respond to the therapeutic model, so the adult must continually repeat. Endless choice becomes endless badgering, and the effects on children's temperaments and expectations are strange. Trained to be demanding customers, very young kids seem like moody, unsatisfied adolescents. Older kids become emotionally brittle, talking constantly and crying easily. In my experience, the differences between kids who have grown up in elite child care of this sort and other children are sharp.

Many parents no longer command traditional authority over their children—because they're not authoritative and don't spend enough time with them. Even outside of child care, many pay others to be in charge of their kids through swimming lessons, "kindermusik" classes, camps, and commercial birthday parties.

The adults who *do* spend time with their children are part of the service economy: The children are their "customers," while the unseen parents are their bosses. I can tell you that kids are aware of the power lines in this arrangement. "My mother pays you," a five-year-old boy at my center told a teacher who tried to make him clean up toys.

Parents in today's expensive child care, I learned, never ask the question that middle-class parents used to ask of adults who'd been watching their children: "Did he behave?" Instead, they ask, "What kind of day did he have?" (In other words, "What did you provide for him?") As paying customers, they feel entitled to service.

They aren't doing their children—or themselves—any favors.

Brian Connelly is a writer living in Pittsburgh.

The Rigors of Sleep

by Marilyn Penn

NEW YORK, NEW YORK, MAY 2002: Midlife hits everyone with a different set of blues. Some people lament a departed waist and the arrival of its surrogate: a pair of well-defined love handles. Others have to contend with mate separation, empty-nest syndrome, imminent retirement, or the almost universal disillusionment about one's self, partner, child, parent, or general lot in life.

In my case, sleep became the battleground for working out my problems. Then, perversely, sleep itself became my biggest problem.

Somewhere around age 50, I began to perform the following activities while asleep: snore, grind my teeth, tense my shoulders, stiffen my neck, shorten my spine, cramp my feet, inflame my sweat glands, provoke my bladder, and wrestle with my pillow. These exercises left me putty-faced and deeply creviced every morning.

And that was just the physical part. Always prone to nightmares, I found that as soon as I shut my eyes I was losing teeth, being abandoned in lunar landscapes, running from serial killers, and continually making heart-stopping mistakes like leaving my daughter in her high chair while I went skiing for the weekend.

Rather than embracing the arms of Morpheus, I seemed to be cross-channeling into the labors of Sisyphus and exhausting my body in the very act of rest. The paradox was that I had no trouble falling asleep, or even staying asleep for several hours—but the longer I slept, the more fatigued I'd feel. I looked forward to wakefulness as respite from my nightly activity. I just couldn't wait to jump out of bed before dawn for a relaxing round of housework.

My husband was a bad sleeper, too, and I began to wonder if our bedroom had unwholesome vibes. Sheepishly, I began asking others about their sleep habits. That's when I discovered that there are *hordes* of people out there who are sleep sufferers. In addition to all of my own symptoms, I was hearing about dry mouths and throats, nasal congestion, itchy bodies, neurasthenic feet, acid reflux, and inordinate hunger pains. Perhaps sleeplessness is the body's quest for relief from these rigors.

Or perhaps the problem lies in our expectations. Programmed to believe that we should all be getting seven hours or more of nightly relaxation, we become disturbed and anxious when the opposite takes place. The truth is, I'm seldom sleepy during the day—I'm just tired when I wake up. Once awake, I feel relieved and energetic, and all aches and pains disappear. But then I'm bombarded by articles about sleep deprivation, talk-show segments on how to get a better night's sleep, and medical warnings about Americans falling asleep at the wheel (not to mention killing their babies by rolling over them in bed). I worry about all of this . . . and then I worry about the fact that worry interferes with quality sleep.

I know that out there in America another support group is waiting to be born. We'll call it "Jacob's Ladder," in honor of the first recorded incident of a man wrestling in his sleep (although most of us battle demons instead of angels, we know the basic feeling). Jacob was wounded during his sleep encounter, but he survived and went on to become a wide-awake patriarch. As he approached midlife, he probably developed arthritis in that injured hip and proceeded to thrash about like the rest of us.

Even though Jacob is our role model, his son Joseph must be considered a sleep troublemaker. It was

Joseph who presumed to interpret dreams, thereby bestowing additional significance upon the state of sleep. Had it not been for him, sleeping might have remained an activity, such as blinking or yawning, that wasn't subject to extreme scrutiny and concern. No one walks around asking his mate, "How are you blinking today?" or "Did you get enough yawns?" No one even knows how many blinks or yawns are appropriate, so we neither worry nor think about it.

Like other successful support groups, Jacob's Ladder will incorporate a 12-step program. I'm not sure what all of these will be yet, but I do know that the first one will mandate No OBSESSING OVER INSOLUBLE SLEEP PROBLEMS. Just as alcoholics must discipline themselves to resist taking a drink, Ladderites will learn to sit among others and bite their tongues before answering the question, "Howdja sleep last night?"

Marilyn Penn has been published in <u>Newsweek</u> and elsewhere.

Wedding Bell Blues

by Blake Hurst

TARKIO, MISSOURI, MAY 2001: I had planned to age in a gradual process, a kind of graceful slide from the summer of my life through a rewarding fall, with winter somewhere far in the future. No sudden changes, just a slow decline into senescence with, finally, a gray and stooped version of myself dispensing wisdom to my many grandchildren on the porch of our home, these wisdom-dispensing sessions taking place mostly in the early fall, because that's the only time of year the weather is bearable here in the Midwest. The rest of the year would be spent among the idle rich in more agreeable climes.

And I was doing okay . . . at least until the spring of this year. Oh yes, my hairline has been receding for a while, my waistline is expanding, and I'm grayer than I'd like. But these changes have been gradual, and not unexpected. Recently, though, things started going downhill fast. It started when the morning paper became blurry. I found myself turning on the TV when I normally would have been reading, and I finally realized that I needed bifocals. Then a trip to the doctor for a sinus infection led to not one but two prescriptions for blood-pressure medication.

Finally, although grandchildren were in my future plans, I really wasn't prepared for the intermediate steps necessary to get to that goal. But I'm preparing myself now, because my daughter Ann, a senior in college, has announced that her boyfriend, Matt, will be joining us at a family gathering. And he'd like the chance to visit with me. Alone.

Now, I guess he could want to talk about the weather or the prospects of his beloved Nebraska Cornhuskers. But I'm afraid that the subject of our conversation is more likely to be my daughter's hand in marriage. Whoa, that was hard to type! I'm not ready for a discussion of such gravity.

Ann has clearly made the most important decision she'll ever make, and the idea that my opinion would influence her is a humorous thought to anyone who knows her. Her beau's bow to tradition is appreciated, though, and as a prospective father-in-law, I'll honor that tradition by observing all the formalities.

Still, as far as I'm concerned, Ann should be preparing for the big basketball game on Friday night, not shopping for rings. She should still be skinny, with crooked teeth and a mop of unruly hair, instead of tall and beautiful, and preparing to move to who knows where with some stranger.

It seems like it was just yesterday that we rushed our baby girl to the hospital with a scary bout of stomach flu, and spent the night trying to keep her attached to the IV line. Just a blink of an eye after that, she won the award for best athlete in her class and threw her retainer in the trash at McDonald's, resulting in the whole family taking part in Dumpster-diving.

We have a picture of both our girls, at about ages six and five, by our bed, where I see it every night. They're squinting into the wind, looking into the distance, far past their dad. You can't freeze life like a snapshot, but I can't look at that picture without wondering where my life has gone. It's all happening entirely too fast, causing greater awareness on my part of passing time than could ever result from the more visible signs of aging.

I just want to tell the world to stop. But it won't, of course, nor should it. Matt is a fine young man, Ann is mature and responsible, and I believe in marriage—

so I should be happy. I can hardly argue that they're too young, since they're older than Julie and I were when we married. So, I *am* happy. Matt has a very good job, Ann will attend graduate school, and there are plans for the production of future repositories of grandfatherly wisdom.

Yup, I'm happy.

Really.

Blake Hurst now has two married daughters.

The Incident
at Mountain Charlie's

by Kevin Josker

TUCSON, ARIZONA, JUNE 2005: In 1972, I was part of the last military draft. A Teletype machine was set up in the student union at the University at Buffalo, where I was enrolled, and lottery numbers were posted as they were pulled. A room full of 19-year-olds awaited their fate: I got number 364—I didn't have to worry about being drafted.

But the next summer I joined the Navy anyway. All of my friends thought I was crazy, stupid, and ignorant. What a waste of a perfectly good draft number!

I became a radar operator in P-3 aircraft, went to the Philippines, and flew over Vietnam doing reconnaissance. I was there for the evacuation in 1976, and I kept track of the desperate boat people fleeing Vietnam. Many disappeared in the South China Sea—their overcrowded, top-heavy fishing boats swamped by the sea or sunk by pirates who attacked at night. The boy from Buffalo turned into a man that year. The realization that I was privileged to grow up in the United States sank in quickly when I witnessed the lengths to which people would go to gain the freedom I took for granted.

After our deployment, we came home to Moffett Field near San Jose. I moved off the base with a couple of friends and lived in Los Gatos, about 20 miles away. In the '70s, young soldiers stuck out like sore thumbs amid our peers, and much of the country did not condone our job choices. Yet Los Gatos was quiet, and people there didn't automatically associate our short hair with the military.

In downtown Los Gatos there was a place called Mountain Charlie's that played lots of Charlie Daniels, Lynyrd Skynyrd, Allman Brothers, and bluegrass records; it also had live music on the weekends. It was our place during off hours.

One night I was standing at the end of the bar listening to some music when a strange girl walked up to me, said, "You must be in the military," called me a "baby killer," and spat in my face.

Now I'd heard of this happening to other people, but I was completely stunned when it happened to me. She turned and walked away indignantly before I could even react. As she rejoined her party at their table, they all had a good laugh, congratulating each other and chalking one up "for the people."

One of the bartenders passed a napkin to me. I wiped my face, as other patrons watched and slowly receded, not knowing what to expect. Then the bartender put his hand on my shoulder and told me to watch. Waitresses and other employees were leading the offenders out of the bar, involuntarily.

My roommate walked over, patted me on the back, and told me to forget it. But I never did. I felt violated, disappointed, angry, frustrated, depressed, and confused. To this day I wonder if that woman really understood what she'd done.

Twenty years later, I interviewed for a job in San Jose. I scheduled the last flight out of the airport so that I'd have time to drive to Los Gatos after the interview and see if Mountain Charlie's was still there. At 3 P.M. I walked through the swinging doors, slowly taking in the nearly unchanged sights, sounds, and smells. I was the only patron.

The bartender looked at me and said that I must be a '70s patron. I laughed and said, "How did you know?"

"We all have the same dreamy look on our faces when we enter this place," he answered. "Auld lang syne, I guess."

I drank a toast to old buddies and started swapping stories. Other customers had come in by this time and were listening to our tale-telling when I told the bartender the "baby killer" story. The guy to my right was so offended that such a thing had happened that he moved to the stool next to me and bought me a drink. Soon other people walked up, apologized for that woman, and thanked me for my service to our country. I left for the airport feeling much better. I buried that ugly episode that afternoon, and can look at it now with detachment.

I'm a wiser and better man for my experiences in the military. I know what honor, courage, and sacrifice really mean. The young Americans now returning from a different war will be changed in similar ways. But they return to a country with a vastly different outlook, and much more understanding and appreciation, than the one I came home to.

Good for them!

This is Kevin Josker's first published article.

About the Editors

Karl Zinsmeister is editor-in-chief of *The American Enterprise*, a national magazine of politics, business, and culture. His other books include two volumes of firsthand war reporting—*Boots on the Ground: A Month with the 82nd Airborne in the Battle for Iraq* and *Dawn over Baghdad: How the U.S. Military Is Using Bullets and Ballots to Remake Iraq*.

Please visit: **TAEmag.com.**

Karina Rollins is a senior editor at *The American Enterprise*.

notes

notes

notes

notes

notes

NBP

We hope you enjoyed this book.
If you'd like additional information, please contact
New Beginnings Press through their distributors:

Hay House, Inc.
P.O. Box 5100
Carlsbad, CA 92018-5100

(760) 431-7695 or **(800) 654-5126**
(760) 431-6948 (fax) or **(800) 650-5115 (fax)**
www.hayhouse.com

Distributed in Australia by:
Hay House Australia Pty. Ltd. • 18/36 Ralph St. • Alexandria
NSW 2015 • *Phone:* 612-9669-4299 • *Fax:* 612-9669-4144
www.hayhouse.com.au

Distributed in the United Kingdom by:
Hay House UK, Ltd. • Unit 62, Canalot Studios
222 Kensal Rd., London W10 5BN • *Phone:* 44-20-8962-1230
Fax: 44-20-8962-1239 • www.hayhouse.co.uk

Distributed in the Republic of South Africa by:
Hay House SA (Pty), Ltd., P.O. Box 990, Witkoppen 2068
Phone/Fax: 27-11-706-6612 • orders@psdprom.co.za

Distributed in Canada by:
Raincoast • 9050 Shaughnessy St., Vancouver, B.C. V6P 6E5
Phone: (604) 323-7100 • *Fax:* (604) 323-2600

Tune in to **www.hayhouseradio.com**™ for the best in
inspirational talk radio featuring top Hay House authors!
And, sign up via the Hay House USA Website to receive the
Hay House online newsletter and stay informed about what's
going on with your favorite authors. You'll receive bimonthly
announcements about: Discounts and Offers, Special Events,
Product Highlights, Free Excerpts, Giveaways, and more!
www.hayhouse.com